WITCHES!

THE ABSOLUTELY TRUE TALE OF DISASTER IN SALEM

ROSALYN SCHANZER

NATIONAL GEOGRAPHIC

WASHINGTON, D.C.

The National Geographic Society is one of the world's largest nonprofit scientific and educational
organizations. Founded in 1888 to "increase and diffuse geographic knowledge," the Society
works to inspire people to care about the planet. National Geographic reflects the world through
its magazines, television programs, films, music and radio, books, DVDs, maps, exhibitions, live
events, school publishing programs, interactive media and merchandise. *National Geographic*
magazine, the Society's official journal, published in English and 33 local-language editions, is
read by more than 38 million people each month. The National Geographic Channel reaches 320
million households in 34 languages in 166 countries. National Geographic Digital Media receives
more than 15 million visitors a month. National Geographic has funded more than 9,400
wscientific research, conservation and exploration projects and supports an education program
promoting geography literacy. For more information, visit nationalgeographic.com.

For more information, please call 1-800-NGS LINE (647-5463)
or write to the following address:
National Geographic Society, 1145 17th Street N.W., Washington, D.C. 20036-4688 U.S.A.

Visit us online at www.nationalgeographic.com/books
For librarians and teachers: www.ngchildrensbooks.org
More for kids from National Geographic: kids.nationalgeographic.com

For information about special discounts for bulk purchases, please contact
National Geographic Books Special Sales: ngspecsales@ngs.org

For rights or permissions inquiries, please contact
National Geographic Books Subsidiary Rights: ngbookrights@ngs.org

Book design by David M. Seager. Text is set in Caslon Antique and P22 Franklin Caslon.

Library of Congress Cataloging-in-Publication Data

Schanzer, Rosalyn.
Witches! : the absolutely true tale of disaster in Salem / by Roaslyn Schanzer.
p. cm.
Includes bibliographical references (p.   ) and index.
ISBN 978-1-4263-0869-7 (hardcover) – ISBN 978-1-4263-0870-3 (library edition) – ISBN 978-1-4263-0888-8 (e-book)
1. Witchcraft–Massachusetts–Salem–History. 2. Salem (Mass.)–Church history. 3. Puritans–Massachusetts–Salem–History.
I. Title.
BF1576.S33 2011
133.4'3097445–dc22
2011012989

Printed in the United States of America
11/WOR-CML/1

TABLE OF CONTENTS

A FEW ACCUSED WITCHES
IN ORDER OF APPEARANCE

TITUBA
Slave of Salem Village's
Reverend Samuel Parris

SARAH GOOD
Homeless beggar with two
young children

DORCAS GOOD
Sarah Good's 4-year-old
daughter

SARAH OSBORN
A bedridden old
woman

MARTHA & GILES CORY
Woman who has an illegitimate son and her
80-year-old husband, a farmer

ELIZABETH & JOHN PROCTOR
A successful tavern keeper
and his wife

REBECCA NURSE
Well-loved 71-year-old
grandmother

GEORGE JACOBS SR.
80-year-old farmer with
rheumatism

THREE DOGS
Accused of belonging to
the Devil

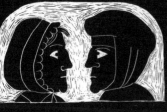

SARAH CLOYSE & MARY EASTY
Rebecca Nurse's highly
respectable sisters

REVEREND GEORGE BURROUGHS
Former minister of Salem Village
who lives in Wells, Maine

BRIDGET BISHOP
Tavern keeper from Salem Town,
wears a red bodice, married 3 times

PHILIP & MARY ENGLISH
Extremely wealthy merchant
and his pregnant wife

SOME AFFLICTED ACCUSERS & OTHER WITCH HUNTERS

REVEREND SAMUEL PARRIS
Salem Village's controversial
minister

INCREASE & COTTON MATHER
Father and son ministers from Boston who write
terrifying books about witchcraft

BETTY PARRIS
Afflicted accuser, 9-year-old
daughter of Reverend Parris

ABIGAIL WILLIAMS
Afflicted accuser, 11-year-old
orphaned niece of Reverend Parris

ANN PUTNAM JR.
Afflicted accuser,
12-year-old friend of Betty
and Abigail

THOMAS PUTNAM
Accuser, strongest supporter of
Reverend Samuel Parris, father of
Ann Putnam Jr.

ELIZABETH HUBBARD
Afflicted accuser, 17-year-old
niece of a physician who blames
witches for the afflictions

JOHN HATHORN
Interrogator during the preliminary
witchcraft investigations

MARY WARREN
Afflicted accuser, 20-year-old servant
of Elizabeth and John Proctor

MARGARET JACOBS
Confessed witch who accused her
grandfather, George Jacobs Sr.

SUSANNA SHELDON
Afflicted accuser, 18-year-old refugee from the
Indian wars

MERCY LEWIS
Afflicted accuser, 19-year-old servant of Ann
Putnam Jr., and Indian attack survivor

WILLIAM PHIPS
Royal Governor
of Massachusetts

WILLIAM STOUGHTON
Chief Justice—Court of
Oyer and Terminer

GEORGE CORWIN
High Sheriff of
Essex County

PREFACE

WITCHES! *For centuries, these horrid creatures have invaded the nightmares of superstitious souls around the world. Who was to blame for causing a terrible, unexplained pain or an untimely death? What if your farm animals fell into a fit and began to dance and roar, or your milk jug shattered before your eyes for no reason, or your child was born deformed? A wicked witch must have been casting spells to harm the innocent or to settle a score.*

In European lore, witches consorted with spirits shaped like animals; vicious cats perhaps, or wild black hogs, or birds. Far more sinister was the idea that witches were the enemies of God—and the agents of Satan himself.

But the most frightening thing of all was this: Anyone could be a witch—your own mother or father, your best friend, your tiny baby brother, or even your dog. And you might never know who was in league with the Devil until it was too late.

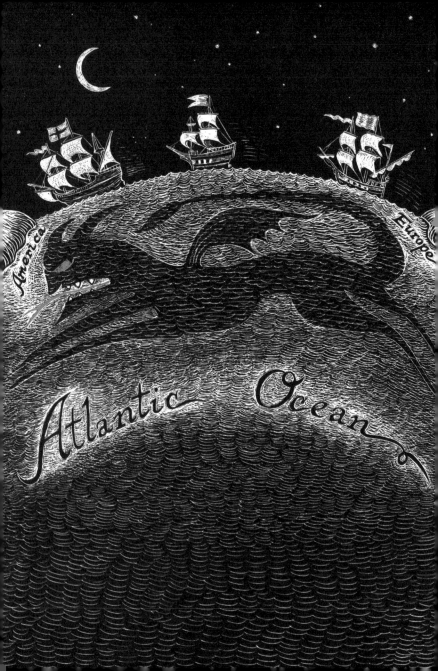

WHEREIN THE STAGE IS SET

cross the wide ocean they came, European emigrants looking for a new beginning on American shores. Many settled in New England, and among these were the Puritans, an English religious sect hoping to live a simple, God-fearing life and to create a heaven on earth. Even before their first ships set sail for the port of Salem Town, Massachusetts, in 1629, they had bucked the British tide for years in an effort to purify their church, banishing every trace of pomp and circumstance, from priestly vestments and music to incense and colorful stained glass windows.

Yet with all their fine intentions, the voyagers had brought along a stowaway from their former home—a terrifying, ancient idea fated to wreak havoc in their new land. For the Puritans believed in the existence of two entirely different worlds.

The first of these was the Natural World of human beings and everything else we can see or touch or feel. But rooted deep within the Puritans' souls like some strange invasive weed lurked their belief in a second world, an Invisible World swarming with shadowy apparitions and unearthly phantoms of the air.

To be sure, many spirits in this hidden world were wondrous and benevolent. These winged seraphs were the angels of the Lord, who wished only to protect the living or offer advice in times of trouble. But the Invisible World was perilous too, boiling over with fire and brimstone and legions of evil, malicious creatures. So great was their power that they dared to do battle with God's own angels—and the leader of them all was the Devil, a fallen angel himself!

The Devil's malice was most fierce and most cunning when he waged his wicked wars upon God's Children. To that end, he and his brutes, each one a fiend to the bone, formed a vicious army determined to destroy everything that was good in the Natural World. Among Satan's soldiers were foul-smelling souls of the dead, horrid imps of darkness cleverly disguised as animals, and a ghastly knot of demonic fallen angels who denounced the word of God. And perhaps worst of all were the Devil's witches, for they could hide in the land of mortals to cast their spells upon the innocent.

The Puritans were terrified by this Invisible World, whose hideous creatures were every bit as real to them as their own families, neighbors, and farm animals.

Puritan ministers preached that it was God Almighty who controlled these two worlds, and he was fearsome, vengeful, and easy to displease. Though pious Children of the Lord might be rewarded for good behavior, any sinners who did not obey his laws would be punished along with their entire communities. And here's a surprise: Because God was all-powerful, even the Devil and the demons and the witches were under his control. Satan was truly an instrument of the Lord, for it was God himself who loosened the Devil's chains and allowed this horrid creature to mete out God's punishments.

The Puritans trusted that God did everything for a reason, so they took note of the things happening all around them in the belief that he was sending them signs. And as more and more Puritans spread outward from Salem Town, Massachusetts, to build new towns and farms on Indian territory in Maine and New Hampshire, they discovered a multitude of horrifying signs in America—if only anyone could figure out what they meant!

∽ EARTHQUAKES, DROUGHTS, FIRES, and a PLAGUE OF FLIES ravaged the land.

∽ Fierce HURRICANES swept the seas, obliterating every ship in their path.

∽ Blazing COMETS and SHOOTING STARS streaked across the sky, eclipses blocked out the sun, and the colorful lights of the AURORA BOREALIS danced and swirled through the night.

∽ There was DISEASE aplenty: Deadly smallpox epidemics devastated entire populations, while malaria, yellow fever, measles, and other maladies tormented young and old alike.

∽ Two fearsome WARS between the English and the Indians raged for 14 years all throughout New England, destroying farms and villages on both sides and causing terrified Puritans to flee back to the relative safety of Salem Town and a nearby farming community called Salem Village.

To the Puritans, every one of these signs seemed to signal God's wrath.

And God's wrath was exactly what was troubling Reverend Samuel Parris, the Puritan minister of little Salem Village.

It was early January 1692, and every member of the Parris household was shivering with cold. Each night the water inside their house would turn to solid ice as a shrieking wind howled on, whistling through cracks in their walls and floorboards. Reverend Parris was extremely upset, and there were three reasons why.

First was the firewood promised in his contract with the Salem Village church (there was hardly any left).

Second was his promised pay (there wasn't any). A church committee of wealthy merchants and landholders in Salem Village disapproved of Reverend Parris and had just voted down a tax that was supposed to provide the money. Parris was enraged and began making fiery sermons, thundering from his pulpit that these "Wicked and Reprobate men" had joined forces with the Devil to destroy the Puritan religion and all that it stood for. ". . . Here are but two parties in the world," Parris proclaimed, "the Lamb and his followers, and the dragon and his followers. Everyone is on one side or the other."

But the third reason was by far the worst of all. Something was terribly wrong with the reverend's nine-year-old daughter, Betty, and his orphaned eleven-year-old niece, Abigail Williams.

Normally, the Parris household would have been a hive of activity filled with eight hard-working people. Besides Parris, who was forever sitting beneath his map of the world to write yet another terrifying sermon, there was his good-hearted but somewhat frail wife, Elizabeth. There were the couple's three children—Thomas, age 10; Betty; and little Susannah, 4 years old—and there was Parris's niece, Abigail.

In addition, Parris owned two slaves—Tituba, an Arawak Indian woman who was kidnapped by a slave runner in South America when she was a young child, and her husband, John Indian, who had been married to Tituba for the past three years. Tituba had helped raise the Parris children ever since they were babies.

If all had been well during this unusually harsh winter, Betty and Abigail would have spent most of their time working together indoors. There was not much playtime in Salem Village; children were expected to help out the same as adults from the time they were about four or five years old. So when there were chores to do (and there were always chores to do—except on Sunday, when everyone was in church), the two girls might have knit some warm socks, boiled laundry in their enormous fireplace, swept ashes off the floors, ladled out porridge for breakfast, or helped make a wild venison pie and some sweet pudding for lunch in their big iron cooking pot. When all this work was done, they could card some wool or linen, twist its fibers into yarn on a wooden spindle, mend torn britches, or even upholster a chair. Of course, they would spend some time studying the Bible and saying their prayers. And if they ever took a break, they might sip some pear or apple cider from large pewter cups.

But that's not what happened one freezing day in January 1692. Not at all. For as winter's sleet and snow heaped higher and higher outside their door, Betty and Abigail began to twitch and choke and contort their bodies into strange abnormal shapes, crouch beneath the furniture, and speak in words that made no sense.

A DIRE DIAGNOSIS

ays passed, but the two girls' frightening symptoms only intensified, even though no one else in the household was getting sick. So Reverend Parris began to wonder. Maybe the children's illness meant that God was sending him a sign. Maybe his congregation had committed some unforgivable sin and was being punished for its own good!

And did the reverend see a second sign of God's wrath? Just one week after the awful fits first struck, and a mere 75 miles to the north, in York, Maine, the Abenaki Indians and their French allies attacked, leaving the town in flames. Even babies, women, and farm animals had been slaughtered. Puritans like Reverend Parris had long believed that Indians were devils and their shamans were witches. He may have wondered if God had unleashed the destroyers to teach his subjects a lesson.

Perhaps Parris had received a third sign as well, for early in February a homeless woman named Sarah Good came knocking at Parris's door, begging for food for her baby and her four-year-old daughter, Dorcas. As Sarah Good turned to go, she muttered something under her breath. Was their gift too small? Were her words curses, the kind that caused crops to fail and livestock to die? The two afflicted girls soon seemed to get much worse.

Parris thought some more and began to wonder if he himself had been the sinner. Had he been lax in his duties as a minister or as a father? Parris prayed and fasted, and so did the rest of his family. He consulted with doctors and tried dosing the girls with every elixir he could find, from parsnip seeds in wine to smelling salts made from blood, ashes, and deer antlers. Nothing worked.

Then an elderly physician named William Griggs, who had lived in Salem Village for perhaps two years, examined Betty and Abigail and declared that they were most certainly "under an Evil Hand." This was the worst of all possible news because it meant that the two girls were BEWITCHED!

Dr. Griggs had good reason to think so.

As early as the 1640s, about 50 years before Betty and Abigail first got sick, settlers in New England had begun to suffer from violent, life-threatening fits. Even farm animals wrestled with these convulsions; many that seemed healthy one day could wind up dead the next. But why? Doctors couldn't find any rational explanation for the victims' bizarre contortions. Nor could they explain people's visions of dark apparitions and bright lights; their temporary paralysis; their blindness and deafness; or their claims that they were being pinched, choked, bitten, scratched, sat upon, or pricked with pins.

Before long, the Puritans began to look for answers in the Invisible World. Was this truly some new dread disease, or could the symptoms have been caused by witches? After all, the Devil's witches could infiltrate the Natural World. If such an invasion had occurred in New England, perhaps these dreadful creatures were working their magic on mere mortals, casting spells and stabbing images of victims from afar to inflict pain, or staring at their prey with a poisonous Evil Eye until they died. Worse yet, witches could be corrupting the innocent, who might join league with the Devil by signing his book of laws just to ease their pain—or bargain away their own immortal souls in exchange for their heart's desire.

That's why in 1641, 1642, and 1655, new laws in Massachusetts and Connecticut proclaimed that witchcraft was a crime punishable by death. The first so-called witch to hang was a healer from Charlestown, Massachusetts, named Margaret Jones. It was said that her mere touch could cause violent pains, deafness, and vomiting, and that she had used witchcraft to kill animals. She was tried and hanged in 1648 during an epidemic of fits. But most cases like hers were thrown out of court for lack of solid evidence or because magistrates and ministers thought the witnesses were delusional or carried a grudge against the accused. Take the case of a New Haven, Connecticut, widow named Elizabeth Godman. In 1655, she was released from jail in spite of one woman's claims that Godman was pinching her and causing dreadful fits that left her boiling hot, freezing cold, and shrieking in pain.

The rash of mysterious fits never disappeared completely, and by the 1680s, rumors about this dread disease were scaring people half to death. Fear spread even farther when a popular father-and-son team of Boston ministers named Increase and Cotton Mather wrote several astonishing books and essays about settlers who were possessed by demons or plagued by witches. One of the most terrifying tales came from Cotton Mather's 1689 best seller, *Memorable Providences*. Everyone flocked in droves to read this story, especially since Mather claimed that he had watched with his own two eyes as every detail unfolded.

In the reverend's book, four children from a pious Boston family were suffering from horrible fits. Their tongues would first be sucked down their own throats, then pulled out upon their chins to a prodigious length. Their jaws would snap out of joint and then clap together like a strong spring lock. They cried that they were being cut with knives, then struck with blows. Their necks were broken! Their heads were twisted almost all the way around! And they would bark like dogs or roar exceedingly loud. These tortures were blamed upon a neighbor, an old Irish Catholic washerwoman named Goody Glover, who was suspected of being a witch. Before long, she was tried in court and hanged by the neck until dead. Surely Reverend Parris and Dr. Griggs knew all about this famous tale.

The day after Dr. Griggs presented his dire diagnosis to the Parris family, Reverend and Mrs. Parris rode off to a lecture. While they were there, they hoped to invite some neighboring ministers to join them in their home for a solemn day of prayer. But as soon as the parents left, the two Parris slaves, Tituba and John Indian, did something that was strictly forbidden. They knew that in New England, people used folk magic all the time to perform cures, even though Puritan ministers railed against it. There were ways to draw out witches—by boiling snippets of children's hair, for example—and the two slaves were apparently so worried about Betty and Abigail that John Indian accepted a set of instructions from their helpful neighbor, Goodwife Mary Sibley, telling how to bake a black magic witchcake.

Carefully following Sibley's recipe, Tituba and John Indian mixed some rye flour with the afflicted girls' urine, patted it into the shape of a cake, and baked it in the ashes of their fireplace. The trick was to feed this magical witchcake to a dog. Ancient European folklore alleged that dogs were the "familiars" of witches. This meant that dogs were actually imps disguised as animals to help witches do their dirty work. When a dog ate a witchcake, the witches' spells were supposed to be broken. Then the victims could reveal the witches' names for all to hear.

But when Reverend Parris and his wife got home and found out about the witchcake, they were absolutely furious. Using black magic was an enormous sin! Though the two slaves were probably just trying to help, black magic could not be tolerated. Parris would later preach that Goodwife Sibley had "a-going to the Devil for help against the Devil."

Betty and Abigail must have been terrified by now; their fits and strange gibbering grew worse, and the contortions of their backs, necks, and arms were frightful to behold. Maybe Parris and his family still had not been pious enough! Parris and the neighboring ministers prayed together. He and his family fasted yet again. And he made sure that everyone in his household doubled their prayers again, too. But the minute a prayer would end, the girls' fits began anew.

So Parris, the other ministers, and certain townsfolk pressed Betty and Abigail hard to reveal the witches' names. Whose evil spirits had ventured forth from the Invisible World to torture them? How could the girls ever get well if the guilty witches were allowed to roam free?

If these two impressionable children were convinced that witches were out to get them, whom should they blame? Maybe their tormentors were the usual suspects, people their family didn't like or respect. Tituba seemed to be a logical choice. Besides making the witchcake, she was a slave, and an Indian slave at that.

After all, everybody the girls knew was convinced that Indians were in league with the Devil. So Betty and Abigail declared that Tituba was a witch and that Tituba's spirit, which was invisible to everybody else but themselves, had been pinching them and pricking them and chasing them around the room.

Before long, they claimed that two other women's spirits had tortured them as well.

First, Betty and Abigail remembered Sarah Good, the muttering beggar woman who had pled for food for her two young children. In Salem Village, nobody liked a beggar, especially an ungrateful, pipe-smoking beggar. She had to be a witch.

And then they pointed the finger at a bedridden old farm woman named Sarah Osborn, whose young second husband used to be her own servant. She had not gone to church for more than a year, and rumor had it that this husband was a wife-beater. Nobody liked Osborn either, especially a certain family called the Putnams, who had fought with her for years over some land and were now leading members of Parris's church. Betty and Abigail claimed they had seen a bird with a human head that turned into Sarah Osborn! She was obviously a despicable witch.

Tituba said she loved Betty and would never have hurt her, but Reverend Parris seemed not to believe a word she said. It was time to take action. So on February 29, 1692, the first official complaints were filed by two Salem Town magistrates, and the three accused witches were arrested.

Word traveled fast. Even as the arrests were taking place, more people began to say they were tormented by fits. And almost every one of them would claim that it was witches—or the witches' spirits—that were torturing them.

The first of these new accusers was a clever 12-year-old girlfriend of Betty and Abigail named Ann Putnam Jr. Ann's parents were the very strongest supporters Reverend Parris had in Salem Village. It seems that Ann was having dreadful fits, and they were all because the spirit of that beggar woman named Sarah Good was pinching her and trying to make her sign the Devil's evil book.

Then a 17-year-old girl named Elizabeth Hubbard claimed she had been chased by a wolf that turned into Sarah Good and attacked by the bedridden old lady, Sarah Osborn. Hubbard happened to be the niece of Dr. Griggs, the very same physician who had first blamed Betty's and Abigail's fits on witchcraft. Not only did Hubbard live in Dr. Griggs's house, but she was friends with Betty and Abigail, too.

CHAPTER THREE

LET THE GRILLING BEGIN

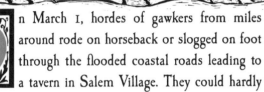

On March 1, hordes of gawkers from miles around rode on horseback or slogged on foot through the flooded coastal roads leading to a tavern in Salem Village. They could hardly wait to find out what would happen at the questioning of the three suspects. Before long, an ugly crowd grew so big that everyone had to move to the church instead.

Today's plan was to question the suspects and decide if they should appear before a grand jury at a later date. If the grand jury determined that there was enough evidence against these three women, they would eventually face a formal trial.

Nobody could be executed for witchcraft (or anything else) before appearing all three times. But accused people could most certainly be sent to prison. In fact, they would be stuck in the jailhouse for a very long time as the process dragged on.

First, the three accused women were examined for witch's marks; did they have warts or bumps anywhere on their bodies that could be used as teats to feed their evil animal familiars? Not a mark was found.

Next, the two magistrates began their interrogation. Only one suspect was brought into the room at a time, but even before the defendants spoke a single word, it was obvious that the magistrates thought all three of them were witches. And it didn't help their cause a bit when all day long the four accusers kept screeching and tumbling around on the floor and crying out that the suspects' spirits were swooping through the air to torture them.

A man named Ezekiel Cheevers wrote down the questions and answers as fast as he could. Of course he already thought the women were guilty, too, as you can tell from his comments.

∽ THE EXAMINATION OF SARAH GOOD ∽

Magistrate John Hathorn (H): *Sarah Good, what evil spirit is your familiar?*
Sarah Good (G): *None!*
H: *Why do you hurt these poor children?*
G: *I do not hurt them. I scorn the very idea.*

H: *Then what creature do you employ to hurt them?*

G: *There is no creature. I am falsely accused!*

H: *Why did you go away muttering from Mr. Parris's house?*

G: *I did not mutter. I thanked him for what he gave my child.*

Recorder's note: *Hathorn asked the children to look upon Sarah Good and see if this were the person who had hurt them, and so they said this was one of the persons that did torment them. Presently they were all tormented by fits.*

H: *Sarah Good, do you not see what you have done? Why don't you tell us the truth? Who do you serve?*

G: *I serve God. The same God that made heaven and earth!*

Recorder's note: *Her answers were given in a very wicked, spiteful manner, retorting against the authority with foul and abusive words and many lies. Her husband said that he was afraid she either was a witch or would become one very quickly. "And indeed," said he, "I may say with tears that she is an enemy to all that is good."*

∽ THE EXAMINATION OF SARAH OSBORN ∽

The girls in the courtroom announced that Sarah Osborn was one of the three witches who were torturing them in this very room. Then they began to shake violently and tumbled to the floor.

When grilled by the furious magistrate, Osborn cried that she had never seen an evil spirit or met with the Devil in her life. She was not tormenting anyone!

"Sarah Good sayeth it was you that hurt the children," argued the magistrate.

"I have not seen her for two years," Osborn replied, insisting that for all she knew, the Devil had the power to make himself look exactly like her. Then he could go around in her shape to attack the girls, but she would have to take the blame.

Three people reported that the bedridden woman thought she was more likely to be the victim of witchcraft than to be a witch herself. When asked to explain, Osborn replied that she had dreamed she saw a black Indian who pinched her and pulled her to the door. Hathorn was not impressed. Implying that she was unfaithful to God, he asked why Osborn hadn't come to church for the past two years. "Alas! I have been sick and not able to go," she cried.

◦ THE EXAMINATION OF TITUBA ◦

The afflicted girls again began to writhe around, screech, and howl when the slave Tituba's turn came to be questioned. At first she said she was completely innocent and that she and the children would never hurt each other. But a little later, she completely changed her tune and confessed that she was guilty!

The recorder who wrote down everyone's testimony didn't bother to say so, but it's possible that the questioning stopped for a while and then started up again after a break, because many months later Tituba would reveal that she had lied when she told the court she was a witch. She claimed Reverend Parris had beaten her to make her confess and to make sure that she accused the two women Parris called her "sister-witches." He even threatened not to pay any of the fees required to get her out of jail unless she told the magistrates that she was guilty. Tituba must have followed her master's orders:

Magistrate (M): *What doth the Devil look like?*
Tituba (T): *Like a man. Yesterday he told me to serve him & I told him no, I would not do such a thing.*

Tituba charged that Sarah Osborn and Sarah Good were

torturing the children and wanted her to hurt them, too. And she said she had seen two more witches from Boston just last night when she was cleaning. They told her she had to hurt the children, and if she refused they would hurt her themselves. At first she agreed to hurt Betty and Abigail, but afterward she was very sorry and told the women she wouldn't do it any more.

> T: *The creature that looked like a man came to me just as I was going to sleep. He said he would kill the children and they would never get well if I would not serve him.*
> M: *What other creatures hath appeared to you?*
> T: *Sometimes a hog. Four times a great black dog who told me to serve him. I told him I was afraid, then he told me he would do worse tortures unto me.*

Tituba said that the man had pretty things and offered her a little yellow bird if she would become his servant. Then he sent her two cats: one red and one black and as big as a dog. But when she said her prayers and tried not to pinch Betty and Abigail, the cats scratched at her eyes, pulled her across the room, and almost threw her into the fire. Tituba felt even worse when the man appeared with Dr. Griggs's niece and made her pinch this girl, too.

> M: *Did you ever go along with these women Sarah Good and Sarah Osborn?*
>
> T: *Yes, they are very strong & pulled me & made me go with them up to Mr. Putnam's house to hurt his Child. The man pulled me, too. But I am sorry.*
>
> M: *How did you get there?*
>
> T: *We Rode upon a stick with Good & Osborn sitting behind me & taking hold of one another. I Saw no trees nor path, but was presently there. They Told me I must kill Thomas Putnam's Child with the knife.*

Ann Putnam Jr. confirmed Tituba's story, saying that they would have made Tituba cut off her own head if the slave refused to kill her.

Then, said Tituba, Good had tried to give her the yellow bird or a cat. Tituba refused to take them, though she wished she could give the pretty bird to the children.

> M: *What did Osborn have?*
>
> T: *She hath two creatures. One hath wings & two*

*Legs & a head like a woman's. The other thing
was all over hairy, all the face was hairy &
had a long nose & I don't know what it is. It was
about two or three feet high & walked upright
like a man, and at night it stood before the fire in
Mr. Parris's hall.*

B ack to jail went the three women. Good was first sent to
a prison in the town of Ipswich. She even had to bring
along her tiny infant, and as she rode away seated sideways
on a horse behind her guard, she swore that she was innocent,
tried three times to escape (once bloodying her arm), and
then tried to kill herself.

Jailers were allowed to question people in prison whenever
they felt like it, so Tituba and Osborn were questioned all
over again in the Salem jail, a dank, filthy dungeon full of rats,
where women were strip-searched so the guards could look
for witch's marks, and where food and water were withheld or
prisoners were tortured in other ways to make them confess.

Even though Tituba followed Parris's orders by claiming
to be a witch, he still hadn't paid her jail fees. Tituba told
the guards that she had been forced to stick herself with a
pin in order to sign the Devil's book with her own blood,

and when she was examined, fresh wounds were found on her body. That's when she claimed Good and Osborn were torturing her out of spite for telling the court they were witches. The magistrates and jailers all believed her. In fact, they thought she was very brave. (Some people thought Tituba's wounds were the Devil's work. Others later claimed that she bore old scars from Spanish cruelty when she was captured as a child. But did these fresh wounds really come from Parris's beating?)

Of course Osborn still maintained her innocence. And in a few days, Good and her baby were sent to Salem's jail, too, where both Good and Osborn were shackled to the wall with heavy chains.

On March 7, all three suspects were transported to another filthy, lice-ridden jail in far-off Boston, where they would be charged a fee for every single day of their stay whether they were guilty or not. They also had to pay for their own shackles. If you were imprisoned in those days, you had to pay a great many fees, even to the very jailers who tortured you, and even if you had no money. Otherwise you could never be set free. Since Tituba had confessed and her young accusers no longer claimed to see her specter, she didn't have to wear chains or go to trial, but until she could pay her jail fees, she most certainly had to stay in prison.

CHAPTER FOUR

WITCH HUNT!

o did the afflicted girls' fits stop once the suspected witches were safely under lock and key? Not on your life. And almost every day, more and more people claimed that they were under attack. Those first three arrests had marked a tipping point; the witch hunt would now begin in earnest.

By March, practically everyone was starting to panic. As skies faded from gray to black on the night that Tituba, Good, and Osborn were sent back to jail, two men thought they saw a shadowy beast crouch down upon the ground and then spring up and up into the sky, where it split apart into the three spirits of the jailed women . . . and vanished!

The very next night, one of these terrified fellows was followed by an enormous white dog. He raced home to his bedroom, slammed the door, and dived under the covers to hide, but just then a large gray cat appeared in a ball of light right in the middle of the bed. And the second man thought he kicked Good's spirit off of his own bed.

Dr. Griggs's niece, Elizabeth Hubbard, cried out that she was being stabbed by the furious spirit of Good, who stood atop her uncle's table "with all her naked breast, and bare footed and bare legged. Oh nasty slut," yelled Hubbard. "If I had something, I would kill her!" Nobody else in the room saw a thing on the table, but Elizabeth's uncle grabbed up his cane at once and swung it valiantly through the air in an attempt to smite the invisible witch. "You have hit her right across the back!" Hubbard exclaimed.

Then Ann Putnam Jr. singled out three more witches:

First was the spitfire spirit of little Dorcas Good, Sarah Good's four-year-old daughter, who supposedly used inhuman strength to pinch Ann, to choke her, and to try to make her sign the Devil's book.

Next, Ann accused a Gospel Woman who was a member of the village church. Her name was Martha Cory. Gospel Women were reputed to be the most zealous church members of all. But even though Cory was a well-liked member of the Puritan religious elite, certain people still disapproved of her because she had once borne an illegitimate mulatto son.

Now she had made a major mistake; she had told people she thought the witch accusations were nonsense.

Martha was the second wife of an 80-year-old farmer named Giles Cory, and she had fought to keep him from going to watch the questioning of Good, Osborn, and Tituba by taking the saddle right off his horse. The cantankerous old man didn't care—he went anyway.

When church deacon Edward Putnam (Ann's uncle) and courtroom scribe Ezekiel Cheevers went to Martha Cory's house to question her, she said, "I know what you have come for. You are come to talk with me about being a witch, but I am none. I cannot help people talking about me." But Ann soon exclaimed that Martha was trying to make her bite off her own tongue, that an invisible yellow bird was sucking a spot between Martha's fingers, and that she had seen a spectral man being roasted on a spit by a spectral Martha Cory!

The third witch Ann incriminated was Elizabeth Proctor, who had been under suspicion for years because her grandmother was supposed to have been a witch.

And who else would rake coals over the reputations of Martha Cory, Elizabeth Proctor, and even Elizabeth's husband, a big burly tavern keeper named John Proctor? It was the Proctors' very own 20-year-old servant, Mary Warren.

Now why would she do that? Was she truly ill? Was she terrified by dark shadows in her chambers? Or was she was out for revenge against her hot-tempered master? Warren had been having (or faking) fits at earlier hearings and claimed that she was afflicted by the specters of Martha Cory and John Proctor. Proctor was so furious at his servant for incriminating innocent people that he had threatened to thrust hot tongs down her throat.

From the very beginning, John had never believed that anyone was a witch, and he thought the self-proclaimed afflicted people should be sent to the whipping post. His attitude infuriated Betty's father, Reverend Parris; Ann's father, Thomas Putnam; and other people who lived with the afflicted. John and Elizabeth Proctor had five children together. Two months after the Proctors were arrested, one of their daughters and two of their sons were taken into custody, too.

The next person to join the growing list of accusers was Ann Putnam Jr.'s 19-year-old servant, Mercy Lewis. After taking care of Ann for two weeks, Lewis started having fits herself. She was being choked! Blinded! Stuck with pins! Pulled by strong forces into a blazing fireplace! And Lewis said it was all the fault of Martha Cory, the very same Gospel

Woman that Ann had already accused. Like Ann, Lewis claimed that she saw Martha Cory's spirit roasting a spectral man on a spit inside her fireplace. When Lewis struck at Cory's spirit with a stick, she suffered "grevious pane" herself, supposedly because the spirit was hitting her with an iron rod.

And besides Martha Cory, wealthy Elizabeth Proctor was out to bewitch Lewis. too. Or so Lewis said. Could the girls have really seen such spirits? Or did they get their story from Cotton Mather's scary book? (Mather had written that an 11-year-old boy said he was roasted on a spit by a witch back in 1688.) Or was Lewis remembering what she saw or heard about during the Indian wars when she used to live in Maine? The Wabanaki Indians had supposedly roasted captive settlers alive over slow fires then. Or was another kind of mischief afoot?

On Saturday, March 19, the high sheriff of Essex County arrested Goodwife Martha Cory. When she was questioned two days later, Judge Hathorn grilled her harshly from the start, constantly accusing her of lying.

> Cory: *Pray give me leave to go to prayer.*
> Hathorn: *We do not send for you to go to prayer,*
> *but to tell me why you hurt these [children].*

Cory: *I am an innocent person: I never had*
       anything to do with witchcraft since I was
       born. I am a Gospel Woman.

At that, Ann Putnam Jr. cried out that Cory was no Gospel Woman, she was a Gospel Witch! By now, witnesses Abigail Williams, Elizabeth Hubbard, Mercy Lewis, Ann Putnam Jr., and her mother, Ann Putnam Sr., were screaming at the top of their lungs and writhing around in agony at Cory's every move. If Cory so much as bit her lip, they bit their own lips and showed bite marks and scratches on their arms and wrists, too, saying that Cory's invisible powers had made them do it. And if Cory so much as wrung her hands when they accused her, they cried out that she had bruised them by making them wring their own hands. A woman named Mrs. Pope threw a shoe at Cory, and it hit her in the head.

Ann claimed she had seen Cory praying to the Devil one night outside her window. Then the afflicted girls said they could hear a drum calling all the witches to gather right outside of the meetinghouse. Even Martha's own husband, Giles Cory, testified against her, blaming her for some very strange things.

It seems that the previous week he had fetched an ox that was lost in the woods, but it promptly lay down in his yard and couldn't get up. It just dragged its rear end as if it had been shot in the hip. Before long, though, it got up on its own. Then his cat fell ill all of a sudden and he thought it would die for sure, so his wife told him to knock it in the head. He would not! And just as suddenly, that cat got well. Besides, he said, his wife liked to stay up after he went to bed. He even saw her kneeling in front of the fireplace as if she was saying a prayer, but he heard not a word.

Right about that time the children cried out that a yellow bird was sitting on Martha. When Magistrate Hathorn asked her about it, she started to laugh. Back to the Salem jail went Martha.

On March 23, Edward Putnam (Ann Putnam Jr.'s uncle) and a farmer named Henry Keney entered a complaint against a 71-year-old grandmother named Rebecca Nurse, who was sick in bed. Everybody loved and respected Goodwife Nurse, who had raised and educated her eight children to become fine, upstanding adults. Besides, she and her husband, Francis, had always been faithful and loyal to one another and to their family and their religion— how could she possibly be a witch?

Some people thought Rebecca Nurse's mother was a witch, so maybe she was a likely target. But was this

accusation really a way to take revenge against the Nurse family? Rebecca's father had often battled with the Putnam family over their farm boundaries. Besides that, Rebecca's husband had been Salem Town's constable in the 1670s, and way back then, the Putnam family was rich. The Putnams had gotten into a big legal battle with the Porters, another wealthy family, over whose timberland was whose. As constable, Francis Nurse had arbitrated their dispute, and the Putnam family lost out in the end.

In all, 10 of 18 depositions against Rebecca Nurse were signed by Putnams, but 2 of the other accusers had grudges against the Nurse family as well. Francis Nurse was a member of the Salem Village committee that voted against paying Reverend Parris's salary in 1691 in order to drive him out of Salem. And then there was the Putnam family's 19-year-old servant, Mercy Lewis. Of course she always sided with Ann Putnam Jr. when it came to accusing people of witchcraft. But Francis and Rebecca Nurse had enough money to hire another man to take their son's place as a soldier in the Indian war. Though this practice was perfectly legal, Lewis, who was orphaned when her family died fighting in the Indian war, might have resented the Nurse family's good luck.

To make matters even worse for Rebecca and her relatives, both Ann Putnam Jr. and her mother claimed that Nurse's two sisters, Sarah Cloyse and Mary Easty, were also witches (and lots of other accusers chimed in). So if the Putnam family, Reverend Parris, and Lewis were out for revenge, they were about to get it.

Rebecca was taken from her sickbed to appear before the magistrates on March 24. "I can say before my Eternal Father I am innocent, and God will clear my innocency," she testified. A sympathetic audience believed her until the victims claimed to see the Devil and a whole swarm of his familiars whispering in her ear. Next thing you know, they said they spotted Nurse's specter as it zoomed past the meetinghouse, riding upon a pole behind the evil black man. And besides, every time she moved, the girls appeared to be bitten, pinched, bruised, or bent as if their backs were broken. "I cannot help it," cried Goody Nurse. "The Devil may appear in my shape!" Off to the Boston jail she went.

The cold winds of March were fading, but still the chilling accusations flew. During Reverend Parris's church services on Sunday, April 10, Tituba's husband, John Indian, was apparently bitten so hard by the spirit of Sarah Cloyse that he started to bleed. Services got even more interesting when Abigail Williams insisted she saw the specters of Cloyse, Nurse, Cory, and Good—and a shining white male angel who made all the witches tremble.

Claims about the suspects were getting more and more out of hand. The next day in the meetinghouse, Abigail made Cloyse seem like she was an enormously important and ridiculously evil witch. According to Abigail, 40 witches had taken communion together in a pasture by drinking the afflicted girls' own blood. And it was served by the two chief witches, none other than Sarah Cloyse and Sarah Good! After hearing such accusations, the real Sarah Cloyse fainted dead away. "Oh!" proclaimed the afflicted girls, "Her spirit has gone to prison to see her sister Nurse!"

Then several girls blamed the spirits of Elizabeth and John Proctor for yanking up a spectator by her feet and for sitting upon the roof beams to harm the people below.

Every day there were more terrible tales of torment. One of the newly accused witches was Martha Cory's husband, Giles Cory. He was supposed to have used witchcraft against at least nine people. An angry woman swore that "the Specter of Giles Cory Murdered his first wife & would have murdered this wife too if she had not been a Witch . . ."

Then two people testified that Cory participated in "the sacriment" at a gathering of 50 witches. Ann Putnam Jr. called Giles Cory "a dreadfull wizard" who "did torture me a great many times." And whenever he shook his head at the accusers or waved his arms in frustration, all the victims shook their own heads and waved their own arms in apparent pain, crying out that Cory was hurting them grievously from all the way across the room.

Ann's father, Thomas Putnam, got in on the act by writing the judge to report that Ann had seen "a dead man in a Winding Sheet who told her that Giles Cory had Murdered him by Pressing him to Death with his Feet, and the Devil promised He should not be Hanged."

But something very surprising happened on April 19. John Proctor's servant, Mary Warren, said that she had been lying when she accused people of being witches. She claimed that the other girls' fits were faked and that they too had lied when they fingered people for witchcraft. The result? She was accused of being a witch herself.

CHAPTER FIVE

A TORRENT OF EVIL

n late April, a deluge of new accusations spewed forth, spreading like the plague farther and farther away from Salem Village itself to 34 different towns. Between April 20 and April 30, 15 additional complaints were entered into the books, and between May 2 and June 6, 39 more people were charged with witchcraft.

Everyone got into the act. Brothers accused brothers. Neighbors accused neighbors. Parents accused their children, and husbands accused their wives. Accusers claimed they had been scratched and bitten and maimed and pricked and disjointed and bloodied and blinded and deafened by invisible furies that no one else could see. Some poor souls said they had been dragged out of their own bedrooms and forced to soar over the treetops to a secret place where they were pressured to sign the Devil's book of laws.

And worst of all was this crippling fear: Seated directly beside you in your very own church might lurk even more witches cleverly disguised as pious worshipers of the Lord.

The record books named 74 people who said they were attacked by witches, and at least 59 of that 74 were female. These so-called victims were as young as 9 years old and as old as 81 (plus another woman described in court records as being "ancient"). The afflicted accusers were not satisfied by pointing out just one witch either. Almost all of them made lots of complaints that got people arrested. For example, Parris's niece, Abigail Williams, fingered 41 different witches for attacking her; Ann Putnam Jr. accused 53; her servant, Mercy Lewis, blamed 54; and a girl named Mary Walcott, who was Ann's step-cousin, named an astonishing 69 witches.

Besides all those victims, a number of Puritans suffering from fits were not officially listed. Some had confessed that they were witches themselves, some were babies too young to complain, and some were men who never accused any witches of making them sick. Since babies can't fake their symptoms and the men didn't claim they were bewitched, surely some of these victims were actually sick.

All kinds of people were accused of witchcraft. There was a fortune-teller, a man who was a judge in the witch trials, and the governor's own wife. There were three floor sweepers, a folk healer, a pirate, and a physician who practiced "counter-magic." There were weavers and watermen, blacksmiths and bricklayers. And there were slaves, merchants, shoemakers, ministers, and servants. Plus two officers in the militia and plenty of farmers. Even the wealthiest couple in Salem Town did not escape arrest.

Not all of the witches were human beings. A girl accused two dogs of belonging to the Devil and said they could cause fits by simply staring at their victims. They were hanged by the neck without benefit of trial. A third dog was bewitched in the town of Andover, supposedly by the magistrate's own brother, who rode upon its back. This dog was executed, too. The same magistrate had refused to send anyone else to jail when more than 50 people were arrested at one time around May 14. For that reason, he was suspected of being a witch as well, so he and his wife and brother fled.

And what did a witch look or act like? There was a hilly-faced man, a woman with "scragged" teeth, a woman who had catalepsy (which meant that she went into trances and became as rigid as a statue), a crooked-backed woman, and a woman who was "broken in her mind." The age of a witch didn't matter one whit. Those accused of witchcraft ranged from age 4 all the way up to age 90.

Of course the jails were bursting at the seams, and it wasn't a pretty picture. All of these horrible dungeons stank to high heaven. People were questioned mercilessly, and if they didn't give the right answers they were tortured. If someone on the outside couldn't bring food to the prisoners when they were hungry or bring them a blanket when they were freezing or bring them money to pay for their room and board, they were out of luck. What's even worse, many prisoners had to leave their babies and young children at home without a bit of care from an adult or a single scrap of food to eat. And if any adults were still at home, how were they supposed to tend their crops alone, visit their loved ones at a far-off prison, or pay the jail fees—especially if they were poor in the first place?

Despite the crowding, more and more people were funneled into jail every day.

Take Bridget Bishop, for example. People had been calling her a witch for ten years, ever since an African slave named Wonn claimed that her specter had stolen some eggs, spooked a team of horses, and pinched him. Bishop ran a rowdy tavern in Salem Town that catered to sailors and other travelers who went there to spend the night, drink rum, and play the evil game of shuffleboard after the neighbors had gone to bed. Bishop was known for wearing a bright red bodice, and gossip had it that she was a prostitute, too. Worse yet, she was suspected of killing her first husband, had been beaten regularly by her second husband, and quarreled late into the night with her third.

Bishop had never once set foot in Salem Village, but on April 18, she was placed under arrest because her specter had supposedly flown there to torture five Salem Village girls. She was questioned the very next day. First, the girls said she was a witch. Then the magistrate himself accused her of bewitching her first husband to death. Bishop insisted that she knew nothing about such attacks, shaking her head and rolling her eyes in frustration. As usual, the five afflicted girls blamed Bishop's specter when their own heads shook violently back and forth and their own eyes rolled wildly in response.

"I am innocent," Bishop testified. "I never saw these persons before, nor I never was in this place before. I have made no contract with the Devil. I never saw him in my life!" At that, Ann Putnam Jr. shouted out: "She calls the devil her God!"

Recorder Ezekiel Cheevers noted that "two men told her to her face that she is taken in a plain lie. 5 afflicted persons do charge this woman to be the very woman that hurts them . . . all her actions have great influence upon the afflicted persons and they have been tortured by her."

As spring breezes warmed the air of Salem on May 10 and 11, a farmer named George Jacobs Sr. and his grand-daughter Margaret were being questioned by the magistrates when Margaret confessed that she was a witch. Then she testified that her grandfather—and a reverend named George Burroughs—were both wizards. (By May, plenty of people knew that if you confessed, you would be treated much better than suspects who claimed they were innocent. If you named extra suspects, you even got to stay in a nicer part of the jail.)

Now it just so happened that Margaret's grandfather was a toothless, 80-year-old man with rheumatism who could only walk with the aid of two walking sticks. Yet despite his sorry physique, 12 screeching accusers exclaimed that Jacobs's specter had beaten them. Lewis joined the fray: "He did torture me most cruelly by beating me with two sticks and almost put my bones out of joint, but I told him I would not write in his book if he would give me all the world."

This particular testimony made Jacobs laugh out loud in court. When the magistrate asked why, he said: "Because I am falsely accused. Your worships, do all of you think this is true?" he asked incredulously. "I am as innocent as your worships."

Sarah Churchill, George Jacobs's maidservant, had already confessed to being a witch to save her own self. In her desire to be let off the hook, she became Jacobs's strongest accuser. And maybe she had another reason, too. When she had told Jacobs earlier that fits were keeping her from doing any work, he had called her a "bitch witch." Here's what else he said at his hearing:

> George Jacobs: *You tax me for a wizard. You may as well tax me for a buzzard! I have done no harm. The devil can go in any shape.*
> Magistrate: *Not without [your] consent. Why do you not pray in your family?*
> Jacobs: *I cannot read. Burn me or hang me I will stand in the truth of Christ.*

CHAPTER SIX

THE KING OF HELL

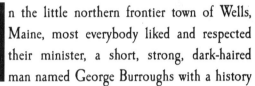

In the little northern frontier town of Wells, Maine, most everybody liked and respected their minister, a short, strong, dark-haired man named George Burroughs with a history of performing heroic deeds for his neighbors. During just the previous summer, for example, he had helped his fellow citizens escape from Indian attacks when warriors snuck up to three nearby towns and laid them all to waste. One of Burroughs's admirers called him "self-denying, generous, and public spirited." Another who knew him well wrote that "he was an able, intelligent, true-minded man; sincere, humble in spirit, devoted as a minister, and generous as a citizen." Also acknowledged as an excellent athlete and a scholar, Burroughs willingly ministered to people of every faith.

Reverend Burroughs had not spent his entire life in Maine. During the early 1680s, he had served two years as the minister of Salem Village and even lived in the same house now occupied by Reverend Parris. Burroughs had headed for Maine after two grave misfortunes befell him in Salem: first, his wife died, and then he got into a bitter dispute with the Putnam family over a debt he owed for her funeral expenses. He had no money because he had never received his salary.

Though it had been ten long years since he had lived in Salem Village, Burroughs was certainly not forgotten, because on April 20, 1692, Thomas Putnam's daughter, Ann, swore that she had seen the apparition of a minister. Ann claimed she had been grievously afraid, crying, "Oh dreadful! dreadful! Here is a minister! Are Ministers witches too? What is your name? He told me that his name was George Burroughs." And the next evening, Reverend Parris's niece Abigail Williams also reported that former minister Burroughs was a wizard!

Two weeks later Burroughs was eating dinner with his family up in Maine, when he heard a ruckus outside his door. In marched Maine's field marshal, Jonathan Partridge, along with a small band of soldiers. Had they come to help the citizens of Wells fight off Indian attacks? Certainly not! They had come to arrest Burroughs, and arrest him they did.

Despite the fact that his neighbors looked up to him as a friend and counselor, Burroughs was immediately escorted all the way down to Salem Town, where he was "Suspected to have Confederacy with the devil."

Even in Salem, where everyone suspected everyone else of witchcraft, people argued fervently about Burroughs's guilt or innocence. One frontier militia leader said he was "a Choice Child of god, and God would Clear up his Innocency." Others thought he was a wife-beater. And yet another swore he had an Evil Eye and "he was the Cheife of all the persons accused for witchcraft or the Ring Leader of them."

By July, a 15-year-old girl from Andover named Mary Lacy Jr., who had confessed that she was a witch, would claim that she had flown to a secret communion where 77 witches were drinking blood and eating blood-colored bread. It was there that she saw a woman named Martha Carrier, also from Andover, who was supposed to have killed 13 people and was now Hell's own Queen. And it was there, too, that she saw the Devil make a promise: Reverend George Burroughs would soon be crowned the King of Hell.

Burroughs was examined several times in front of enormous crowds between the day of his first witchcraft investigation on May 9 and his final official trial in Salem

Town on August 5. At least 30 accusers would pile up a mountain of sworn testimony against him. What did they say? Some truly amazing things.

Ann Putnam Jr. said, "He told me he had had three wives: and that he had bewitched the first Two of them to death: and he bewitched a great many soldiers to death at the eastward." These soldiers had died three or four years earlier during battles they lost against the Indians, and some of Burroughs's detractors insisted that he was in cahoots with the enemy French and Indian soldiers. Since Puritans thought the Indians were devils, they believed that Burroughs must be in cahoots with the Devil, too. Then Ann said, "He told me that he was above a witch, he was a conjurer." She embellished her story even more later on:

> *...immediately there appeared to me the form*
> *of Two [dead] women in winding sheets; and*
> *they turned their faces towards Mr. Burroughs*
> *and looked very red and angry and told him*
> *that he had been a cruel man to them and*
> *that their blood did cry for vengeance.*

*Then the Two women turned their faces
towards me and looked as pale as a white wall
and told me that they were Mr. Burroughs'
first Two wives and that he had murdered
them: and one told me that he stabbed her
under the left Arm and put a piece of sealing
wax on the wound and she pulled aside the
winding sheet and showed me the place.*

Next, a woman named Mary Toothaker testified that the minister had ordered a convention of 305 witches to pull down the Kingdom of Christ and set up the Kingdom of Satan. Before long, confessed witch after confessed witch claimed that they had been baptized in the name of the Devil by the King of Hell himself, Reverend George Burroughs.

Eighteen-year-old Susannah Sheldon, another refugee from the Indian war on the Maine frontier, said Burroughs threatened that if she wouldn't sign the Devil's book, he would tear her to pieces, starve her to death, and choke her until her vittles gave out. And to scare her even more, he said he killed three children on the frontier, smothered and choked two of his wives to death (their ghosts again agreed), and murdered two of his own children.

Though Burroughs was a short, slender man, some witnesses testified that he possessed superhuman strength that could only come from the Devil. Why, he could put two fingers in the bung holes of enormous barrels of molasses or cider or meat and lift them out of a canoe all by himself! He could put one finger into the seven-foot-long muzzle of a heavy fowling gun and hold the weapon straight out in front of him at arm's length. He could run faster than any horse. He could turn into a gray cat. And a man named Thomas Ruck swore that Burroughs "could tell his thoughts."

But who made the most stunning accusations in the entire case? It was none other than Ann Putnam Jr.'s servant, Mercy Lewis. Unlike most of the young accusers, Lewis knew Burroughs—not from the time he lived in Salem Village, but from the time he spent as the minister of Falmouth, Maine, her hometown.

When Lewis was three years old, Falmouth had been attacked and burned to cinders by Indians, and she and the few members of her family who were still alive had escaped to an island in Casco Bay with Reverend Burroughs's help. Much later, when she was 16 years old, Lewis's parents were killed (possibly right before her eyes) in another battle with the Indians, and she apparently became a servant in Burroughs's household for a short while after that.

Burroughs had escaped from every single Indian attack on the frontier without a scratch. Did Lewis believe he was an ally of the Indians? She thought the Indians were devils, and she certainly wanted to get him in trouble, because this is what she swore under oath on April 3:

On the evening of May 7, before his first hearing had even begun, she had seen the spirit of Burroughs, whom she knew very well. This apparition tortured her horribly over and over again, urging her to sign her name in a mysterious book that he kept in his study. He said he had several books she had never seen, and he could use this one to raise the Devil himself. He told Lewis that the Devil was his servant and said he had even commanded the Devil to bewitch several other teenage girls.

Again he tortured Lewis, threatening to kill her if she told anybody what he had just said and ordering her once more to sign her name in the Devil's book. Though he was shaking her all to pieces, she cried that she would never write in that book even if he killed her.

Then she told a rapt audience what happened two days later:

*Mr. Burroughs carried me up to an exceedingly
high mountain and showed me all the Kingdoms
of the earth and told me he would give them
all to me if I would write in his book, and if I
would not he would throw me down and break
my neck: but I told him they were not his to
give and I would not write if he throwed me
down on 100 pitchforks.*

Upon hearing this testimony, the hideous clamor and screeching of the afflicted girls became so intense that they were removed from the courtroom for their own safety.

CHAPTER SEVEN

OYER & TERMINER

On May 14, Royal Governor of Massachusetts William Phips sailed home to Boston after a long visit to London, only to discover that throngs of people were rotting in jail, awaiting their formal trials for witchcraft. So far, nobody in Massachusetts had set up an official court of law that could sentence witchcraft suspects to death. As the King of England's royal representative in America, Governor Phips took immediate action. He asked his council to nominate some new judges so that he could establish a Court of Oyer and Terminer.* Only then could the fates of all those prisoners be determined.

Governor Phips approved the nominations right away and officially established the court in Boston on the hot,

---

* "*Oyer and Terminer*" *means* "*hear and determine.*"

steamy afternoon of May 27. Not one of the judges was schooled in the law. The few trained lawyers in the Massachusetts Bay Colony had studied law in England, and most of them were so frustrated by the legal process in America that they went back home. The first lawyer trained in America wouldn't even be admitted to study law at Harvard until October 18, 1692, almost five months away. What's more, even back in England, men with very little education sometimes served as justices. English people (including American colonists) accused of criminal acts were not allowed to have a lawyer to defend them in a serious criminal trial, and neither were the accused witches.

The court's new chief justice was a thin-faced Harvard graduate and politician from Dorchester who had been educated to become a minister. Lieutenant Governor William Stoughton, a wealthy, 61-year-old bachelor with long white hair, had inherited a lot of land and had often served as the Massachusetts Bay Colony's chief justice between 1674 and 1686. A staunch Puritan, Stoughton was absolutely unbending about his belief in witchcraft.

These were the other judges:

- Samuel Sewall—*Harvard graduate from Boston, educated for the ministry; merchant and militia officer in the Second Indian War*
- Nathaniel Saltonstall—*Harvard graduate and wealthy gentleman from Haverhill; active militia officer for Essex County during the Second Indian War; justice of the peace*
- Peter Sergeant—*Wealthy Boston gentleman without a profession*
- Wait-Still Winthrop—*Boston physician and active militia leader in the Second Indian War; attended Harvard but did not graduate*
- Jonathan Corwin—*Wealthy merchant and military advisor from Salem; a magistrate during the preliminary witchcraft investigations*
- Bartholomew Gedney—*Owner of a wharf and shipyard in Salem Town, mills north of Casco Bay, and land in Maine; former justice of the peace; magistrate who had occasionally acted as an interrogator during the preliminary witchcraft investigations*

- John Hathorn—*Salem magistrate who often acted as an interrogator during the preliminary witchcraft investigations; military advisor during the Second Indian War*
- John Richards—*Former servant from Boston who worked his way up to become a wealthy merchant and a major in the militia during the Second Indian War*

Back before this new court was formed, almost every single person who had landed in jail had been locked up because of evidence from the Invisible World of spirits. The legal term for this was "spectral evidence," which meant evidence related to supernatural beings that were invisible to everybody except the afflicted accusers. Hardly a scrap of evidence had come from the Natural World of real things that everyone could touch and see.

So how would the judges of the new Court of Oyer and Terminer conduct their trials? Would they do anything differently this time around and get rid of spectral evidence? At Sabbath services in Boston on May 29, three of the new judges listened attentively as their pastor, Samuel Willard, compared the Devil to a roaring lion who could send forth innumerable other devils to devour the innocent. His witches were so cruel and bloody, said the pastor, that it was the judges' duty to use every weapon in the book—including spectral evidence—to see that they were hanged.

To be sure, a number of people had always been leery about the use of spectral evidence in court, and a few brave souls were not afraid to say so out loud. But when the new court was formed, these skeptics were in the minority. The majority still agreed with Willard; to them, spectral evidence provided unvarnished proof that someone was a witch.

And another circumstance did not bode well for the accused witches. Several of the judges had served together on the Maine frontier as councillors or officers during the Second Indian War. The English were losing the war in a big way, often because of the judges' own blunders—blunders that had gotten people killed. But instead of taking the blame, they attributed their defeats to "the awfull Frowne of God," for it was God who had loosened the Devil's chains to let him work his evil deeds upon New Englanders as a punishment for their sins. Therefore all those lost battles—and even the attacks by witches—must have been the fault of sinners in their midst, not the fault of the judges' military errors. Why? If the Puritans had behaved themselves, God would have been on their side, the war would have been won, and witchcraft would never have erupted. To the judges, it apparently made sense to blame the lost battles on witches, who were the Devil's representatives in the Natural World.

It was June 2, 1692, and the time to begin the first formal trial for witchcraft had arrived at last. The first person to be tried was Bridget Bishop, the keeper of Salem Town's rowdy tavern.

Bishop seemed doomed from the start. As she was led from the jail toward the court, she glanced over at an empty church just as something came crashing down inside its walls. The spectators were sure that her spirit had caused all the trouble. This was not a good sign.

The moment Bishop arrived in court and pled innocent, another torrent of accusations poured forth—and nothing had changed from the previous hearings because every single bit of the evidence against her was spectral. One man claimed that Bishop had bewitched his child; he said the boy had been stupefied for 12 years. Another man said that 14 years earlier Bishop had hired him to do some work and paid him well, but by the time he got 15 or 20 yards away from her house, he realized that the money had vanished out of his pocket. Not long after that, the man saw her again, and his wagon "plumped or sunk down into a hole upon plain ground" and his wagon wheel fell off. He even testified that Bishop's spirit had been hopping around on his bed wearing a black cape and hat.

A woman who had given Bishop a tongue lashing for stealing her spoon ten years earlier was convinced that Bishop's specter was trying to drown her. Crazed with fear, she had lost her sanity. Bishop's spirit had supposedly snatched a girl from her spinning wheel and tried to drown her, too. And some people even claimed to have met ghosts who said they were killed when Bishop stared at them with her evil "eye beams." One field hand said he saw Bishop's spirit stealing eggs again and then stared in wonder as she transformed herself into a cat.

Two workers who had repaired Bishop's house testified that they had found some old stuffed dolls called poppits hidden inside a wall. Nobody really knew who owned them, but they were made out of rags and boar bristles, and lots of headless pins had been stuck into them. This was bad news because people had also found pins stuck into the accusers' skin right there in the courtroom. Could Bishop's spirit have put pins into the dolls in her house in order to torture her victims from afar?

But here's the story that sealed her fate. According to Bishop's neighbor, a hairy, black thing with the face of a man,

the body of a monkey, and the feet of a rooster jumped into his window carrying a message from the Devil, who was out to kill him. The neighbor struck at this monster with a stick, but it was like striking thin air. The monster flew out of the window and vanished, so the neighbor ran outside, and there was Bishop walking toward her orchard next door. Some strange force made it impossible for him to move a single step in her direction, and at last he turned around to shut his door. Just then, the beast flew toward him yet again, sprang back, and then flew over an apple tree, flinging dust with its feet against his stomach and scattering apples as it sped away. The man was so terrified that he couldn't even speak for three days.

Apparently only one of the judges, Nathaniel Saltonstall, believed that Bishop was innocent. Chief Justice Stoughton and the rest of the men believed every single detail in this mountain of spectral evidence. So the end had come for Bridget Bishop. She was found guilty and condemned to death.

CHAPTER EIGHT

THE END IS NEAR

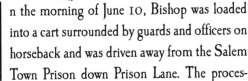

O n the morning of June 10, Bishop was loaded into a cart surrounded by guards and officers on horseback and was driven away from the Salem Town Prison down Prison Lane. The procession then headed toward Salem Village, past crowds of gawking onlookers, and after crossing a bridge, it wound its way to the top of a ledge above a salt marsh. As Bishop continued to proclaim her innocence, guards wrapped her skirt around her feet and tied it tightly at the bottom. Then Essex County's high sheriff, George Corwin, made her stand halfway up a ladder, where she was blindfolded and a noose was placed round her neck. Corwin kicked the ladder out from under her, and the noose jerked tight! She was hanged by the neck until dead.

On the very same day, a man named Thomas Brattle sent a letter to a gentleman in London. He made no mention of Bishop's hanging, but he wrote a few words about the other goings on: "When Witches were Tryed several of them confessed a contract with the Devil by signing his Book, and did express much sorrow for the same, and said the Tempters tormented them till they did it."

This was important because by now so many people who were accused of witchcraft had figured out that they would not be hanged if they confessed. Like Reverend Parris's slave Tituba, all they had to do was to say they were sorry. In the end, 49 people confessed that they were witches.

The next part of Brattle's letter revealed some foolish shenanigans going on in court:

At the time of the Examinations, before hundreds of Witnesses, strange Pranks were played; sometimes the afflicted took Pins out of their own Clothes and thrust them into their flesh. Many of these pins were taken out again by the Judges own hands. Thorns also were thrust into their flesh. The accusers were sometimes struck dumb, deaf, blind, and sometimes lay as if they were dead for a while, and all of these things were foreseen and declared by the afflicted just before it was done.

There were two Girls, about 12 or 13 years of age, who foresaw all that was done and were therefore called the Visionary Girls; they would say, Now he, or she, or they, are going to bite or pinch the Indian; and all there present in Court saw the visible marks on the Indians arms; they would also cry out, Now look, look, they are going to bind a certain person's Legs, and all present saw the same person fall with her Legs twisted in an extra-ordinary manner;

Now say they, we shall all fall, and immediately 7 or 8 of the afflicted fell down, with terrible shrieks and outcries even though the Witch was tied up with a Cord and the afflicted Indian Servant was on his way home, (being about 2 or 3 miles out of town). Many Murders are supposed to be committed in this way, for these Girls, and others of the afflicted, say they can see Coffins and bodies in Shrouds rising up and looking at the accused, crying Vengeance, Vengeance on the Murderers.

On June 15, five days after the hanging, Judge Nathaniel Saltonstall resigned from the court. He had been totally appalled by its proceedings. Apparently a growing number of people were beginning to feel the same way because on that very same day, 14 ministers from 12 different towns presented an important message to the Court of Oyer and Terminer. Entitled "Return of the Several Ministers" and written by famous Boston minister Cotton Mather (the author of that scary 1689 book about children with horrible fits), it stated that spectral evidence should never be used all by itself in court.

Mather believed in the Invisible World, but he also thought the Devil could make himself look exactly like an innocent person whenever he did his evil deeds. That way the Devil could lay the blame on anyone he pleased and they would be wrongly condemned to death. If the new magistrates were to do their duty properly, Mather wrote, they would only punish people for crimes everyone could see with their own two eyes.

Would the chief justice and his fellow judges on the Court of Oyer and Terminer finally read what the document had to say and ban spectral evidence from the courtroom so that the trials could be fair?

The answer is no. The court did NOT abolish spectral evidence. It was obvious from their first trial that, to them, evidence everybody could see was simply not necessary. Before long, Nathaniel Saltonstall, the judge who had resigned, was accused of being a witch himself.

The Court convened again on June 29 for the final trials of these five women:

SUSANNA MARTIN

ELIZABETH HOW

SARAH WILDES

REBECCA NURSE

SARAH GOOD

Witnesses told scores of bizarre tales about the suspects. Their specters had drowned 13 oxen! Twisted a farm hand into a hoop! Turned into a ball of light the size of a bushel basket! Vanished into thin air! Choked a woman with nails and eggs, and choked men in bed or tore them to pieces! One suspect had turned into a black hog at a sinful party and another caused a horse to set a barn on fire. Again, the judges believed every word.

A woman named Goodie Bibber testified that the specter of Rebecca Nurse had pricked her with pins in the courtroom, but Nurse's daughter Sarah testified that she had watched Bibber slip the pins out of her own dress and stab herself with them. The jury found Nurse not guilty. But the minute they heard this news, all of the afflicted accusers made a hideous outcry, amazing the spectators and the judges alike. Chief Justice Stoughton sent out the jury a second time, and when they returned, they pronounced Nurse guilty as charged.

Next up was Sarah Good, and for a change, some evidence from the Natural World came into play, according to Robert Calef, who witnessed the proceedings:

> *At the Trial of Sarah Good, one of the afflicted fell into a Fit, and after coming out of it, she cried out that the Prisoner had stabbed her in the breast with a Knife, and said that the Prisoner had broken the Knife when she stabbed her. Accordingly a piece of a Knife blade was found near the accuser. But immediately someone informed the Court that there was some new evidence. A young Man was called, who produced a Knife Handle and*

part of the Blade. The Court saw that it came from the same knife, and upon being questioned, the young Man affirmed that yesterday he happened to break that Knife, and that he cast away the upper part, and this afflicted person was watching when he did it.

Chief Justice Stoughton simply told the accuser to be honest from now on. He had already decided Good was guilty, and the use of false evidence did not matter.

It was the morning of July 19, just one day after Indian raiders had killed several people and kidnapped a three-year-old boy not too far north of Salem Village. The weather was hot and dry, dry, dry on this hanging day for the five condemned witches. As they rode toward Gallows Hill, each of them prayed fervently that God would prove their innocence.

Susanna Martin, a tiny, 70-year-old widow, had laughed at her accusers in court and thought they might be witches themselves. When asked if she had any compassion for the people beset by fits, she said, "No, I have none." Elizabeth How had exclaimed, "If it was the last moment I was to live, God knows I am innocent of anything in this nature." And most of the accusations against Sarah Wildes had been about things that supposedly happened 15 or 20 years earlier.

Salem Town clergyman Nicholas Noyes, the official minister of the trials, told Good he knew she was a witch and tried to get her to make a last-minute confession. Good was furious. "You are a lyer," she exclaimed. "I am no more a Witch than you are a Wizard; and if you take away my Life, God will give you Blood to drink!" Legend has it that 25 years later, Reverend Noyes died of a hemorrhage, choking on his own blood.

The women were buried near the hanging site, but as soon as darkness fell, Nurse's family uncovered her body and transported it by boat to be reburied on their own home ground.

More people than ever flocked to the hangings on Friday, August 19, mostly because everyone for miles around had come to see Salem Village's former minister, George Burroughs. Five condemned witches would be hanged on that day:

JOHN PROCTOR

JOHN WILLARD

MARTHA CARRIER

GEORGE JACOBS SR.

REVEREND GEORGE BURROUGHS

One convicted witch was excused from being hanged with the rest. Elizabeth Proctor was pregnant, so she was allowed to remain in jail. But her faithful husband was certainly not let off the hook. Huge, energetic, and blunt, John Proctor was the tavern keeper who had been accused by his own maidservant back in April. After punishing his servant for framing innocent people (including himself), and after calling the witch trials a sham, he had become the first male to be accused as a witch. He had strongly defended his wife, too, testifying that "If they [the afflicted girls] were let alone, so we should all be devils and witches." Once jailed, John Proctor had written five Boston ministers to say that all the accused witches were innocent and to describe how torture was being used to make his teenage son William and others confess. Of course his petition did nothing to stop the trials.

John Willard had fled from Salem Village after a warrant was issued for his arrest, and he managed to reach a field he owned 40 miles away before he got caught. During his examination back on May 18, he had said, "I fear not but the Lord in his due time will make me as white as snow." He, too, never confessed, and he approached the gallows with great dignity.

Back in May, when the girls in the courtroom had accused Martha Carrier of murdering 13 people and said she was the Queen of Hell, she had told the judges, "It is a shameful thing that you should mind these folks that are out of their wits." Carrier, a minister's niece, had been jailed along with four of her five children. Her two oldest sons were tortured along with Proctor's son in an effort to make them say their own parents were witches. Carrier's boys adamantly refused to confess or to blame their mother. For being so stubborn, they had their heels tied to their necks until blood gushed out of their noses. Finally, the oldest said he had signed a black man's book, and he accused 19 witches, including his mother. The younger son said he had signed the book, too. He reluctantly named three witches but refused to accuse his mother.

On August 12, a week before 80-year-old George Jacobs Sr. was sent to the gallows, Sheriff George Corwin confiscated everything he owned—off Corwin went with all of Jacobs's cows, pigs, fowls, land, cider, Indian corn, bedding, brass kettles, pewter, furniture, hay, apples, and cider. He also took a horse and even Mrs. Jacobs's wedding ring. This was illegal. The goods that Corwin stole were supposed to support the family of the accused while he was in jail and were to be turned over to the Massachusetts Bay Colony and the King of England only after his death, but the government never saw hide nor hair of the booty and neither did Jacobs's family.

Puritans believed you had to confess your sins before you died if you wanted to save your soul and go to Heaven. On the day of the hanging, John Proctor absolutely refused to confess that he was a witch, but he did ask Reverend Nicholas Noyes to pray with him at the jail. Noyes angrily refused in turn. So when the prisoners reached Gallows Hill, Proctor and Carrier asked Reverend Cotton Mather to pray with them, and he did. Proclaiming their innocence to the end, they prayed that God would forgive them for any other sins and would forgive their accusers too, so that theirs would be the last innocent blood to be shed.

And what about the supposed King of Hell, George Burroughs? Despite the risk of being condemned as witches themselves, 32 highly respectable citizens of Salem Village signed a petition pleading his innocence. It made no difference.

The day before the hangings, Margaret Jacobs had paid a visit to Burroughs to admit she had lied when she accused him along with her grandfather, George Jacobs Sr. She had already officially petitioned Salem's Court to recant her accusations and thereby save their lives, writing that "What I said was altogether false against my grandfather, and Mr. Burroughs . . . [the jailers] told me, if I would not confess, I should be put down into the dungeon and would be hanged, but if I would confess I should have my life." Though she had risked her own life by recanting, it didn't do a bit of good for her grandfather or Burroughs. Margaret begged Burroughs's forgiveness, and it is said that he was kind enough to pray "with and for her."

The hanging of Burroughs is described here by a spectator named Robert Calef:

> *Mr. Burroughs was carried in a cart with the others through the streets of Salem to his execution; when he was upon the ladder, he made a speech for the clearing of his Innocence, with such Solemn and Serious expressions, as were to the Admiration of all present; he concluded by reading the Lords' prayer so well, and with such composedness and fervency of Spirit, that it drew tears from many, and it seemed that the Spectators would hinder the Execution.*

Puritans believed that a true wizard could not possibly say the Lord's Prayer without making a mistake, but Burroughs had recited it perfectly.

The accusers said the black Devil stood and told him what to say. As soon as he stopped speaking, Mr. Cotton Mather, being mounted upon a horse, addressed himself to the People to declare that Burroughs was no ordained minister, and to convince the people of his guilt; saying that the Devil has often been transformed into the Angel of light; and this did somewhat appease the people, and the Executions went on.

When Burroughs was cut down, he was dragged by the halter to a Hole between the rocks, about two foot deep. His shirt and breeches had been pulled off, so an old pair of trousers of one who was Executed was put on his lower parts and he was then put in the hole together with Willard and Carrier. One of his hands and his Chin and a Foot of someone else were left uncovered.

Giles Cory, the cantankerous 80-year-old farmer who had testified against his wife, Martha, appeared at his final hearing on September 16 and pled "not guilty." He refused to put himself on trial by jury, and some people say he had a good reason: Cory knew he wasn't a witch, and he had no intention of confessing in order to be set free. If he went to trial, he would surely be found guilty and all his property would be taken away, leaving his family with nothing.

So perhaps that's why Cory did a very stubborn thing: He decided to "stand mute" and would not utter one single word in court no matter what happened. Under the laws of New England, anyone who refused to talk could not be tried, but the punishment for remaining silent was far worse than being hanged; it was a type of torture known as *peine forte et dure*. This meant that the prisoner would be forced to lie down on his back while more and more weight was piled on top of him until he either agreed to be questioned in court, confessed, or died.

On Monday, September 19, Cory was stripped naked and a big board was set down on top of his chest. Then, as the townsfolk stared, a large number of extremely heavy rocks were piled one by one onto the board. Cory had only one thing to say; he asked to have more weight added so that he could die faster. But it would take two long days for him to breathe his last. Calef, the spectator who had written about Burroughs's hanging, reported a horrible little detail about Cory: "His tongue being forced out of his mouth, the Sheriff with his Cane forced it in again when he was dying. He was the first in New England that was ever pressed to death."

Cory was buried in an unmarked grave by Butts Brook as if he were a suicide. But some people were greatly upset about the way he had died. Public opposition to the witchcraft trials began to pick up speed.

Thursday, September 22, turned out to be the last time anyone would hang on Gallows Hill, but nobody knew it yet. The final victims of the witch hunt were:

MARY EASTY
MARTHA CORY
MARGARET SCOTT
ALICE PARKER
ANN PUDEATOR
WILMOTT REDD
MARY PARKER
SAMUEL WARDWELL

All eight prisoners were jammed into a single cart, which bumped its way uphill toward the gallows. The overburdened vehicle was so heavy that it got stuck in a rut and almost turned over. Rowdy spectators cried out that "the Devil hindered it."

And what were the last words of the condemned? Respectable Mary Easty, a highly intelligent mother of seven children and the sister of Rebecca Nurse, wrote a well-reasoned, humble petition to the governor and judges urging them to rethink their procedures and to stop condemning the innocent.

> *I Petition to your honours not for my own life, for I know I must die, but with the hope that no more Innocent blood may be shed. I do not question that your honours work to the utmost of your Powers to uncover witchcraft and would not be guilty of Innocent blood for the world. But by my own Innocence I know you are working in the wrong way.*
>
> *The Lord knows that I shall honestly say at Heaven's Tribunall seat that I know not the least thing of witchcraft. Therefore I cannot, I dare not lie and by so doing lose my own soul.*

I beg your honors not to deny this humble petition from a poor dying Innocent person and the Lord will bless your endeavors.

Her plea went unheeded.

What about the seven other people on the list? According to spectator Calef, "Martha Cory, protesting her innocency, concluded her life with an eminent prayer upon the ladder." Her husband, Giles Cory, had been pressed to death just two days earlier. And Margaret Scott had been framed by rumors that a dying man said he would never be well as long as she lived. Then there was Alice Parker, who had been accused of bewitching a girl because the girl's father wouldn't mow her grass (Parker's accuser, Mary Warren, received permission from Judge Stoughton to strike Parker for lying, but Warren had a dreadful fit instead).

Ann Pudeator, the wealthiest person to hang, was accused of making a man fall out of a cherry tree and making ointments to use for sorcery. Wilmott Redd was a gruff, unpopular fisherman's wife from Marblehead. Mary Parker had yelled at her husband for going to a tavern and had also been accused of bewitching a sick child. Parker insisted that she was accused because someone else had the same name as hers.

Last came Samuel Wardwell, an eccentric carpenter, fortune-teller, and magician who had at first confessed that he was a wizard and then changed his mind and recanted. When Wardwell tried to declare his innocence on Gallows Hill, smoke from the hangman's pipe set him to coughing. This prompted the afflicted girls to declare that "the Devil hindered him with smoak."

As usual, hard-nosed Reverend Noyes had not one bit of sympathy for the people who were hanged. "What a sad thing it is to see eight firebrands of Hell hanging there," he proclaimed. About that time, it began to pour down rain.

CHAPTER NINE

THE END IS HERE

s the cool winds of autumn blew into New England, it became obvious that change was in the air. More and more people were starting to realize that the innocent were being executed because of hearsay, malicious gossip, and invisible evidence. Some people even wondered whether the accusers were witches themselves, especially since they said they could talk so easily with the Devil and because they sometimes contradicted their own stories.

Far too many fine upstanding Puritans from the best families were being packed off to jail. Besides that, the main accusers seemed perfectly healthy outside of the courtroom, and the sheer number of suspects was so high that it was impossible to believe this many people could all be witches.

A Beverly, Massachusetts, minister named John Hale said it best: "It cannot be imagined that in a place of so much knowledge, so many in so small compass of land should abominably leap into the Devil's lap at once."

What's more, every single one of the 19 people who were hanged denied the crime of witchcraft right up until the moment they died. If these denials had been a pack of lies, God would never allow their souls to enter heaven, and the accused people knew it. Since nobody wants to go to Hell for lying about being a witch, surely this meant that none of them was guilty. Until now, many townsfolk who thought the trials were unfair had been afraid to say a word for fear of being accused themselves. But it was becoming quite clear that unless the trials were stopped, an entire generation of innocent Puritans could be condemned as witches.

On October 3, Boston Reverend Increase Mather preached a sermon arguing against the witch hunts. He agreed with his son Cotton that the Devil could make himself look exactly like any innocent person he chose. But Increase added that the Devil could play his dirty tricks without a person's permission. (The judges had always claimed that the Devil needed a person's permission before he could use that person's likeness as a disguise.) The upshot was that Increase thought it could be the Devil, not the accused people, who was causing all the trouble. Like Cotton, he again urged the courts to exclude every bit of spectral evidence from now on, saying it would be "better that ten suspected witches should escape than one innocent person should be condemned."

On October 6, six young suspects in the Salem prison were released on bail. This was something entirely new.

On October 8, eight powerful men (a former governor and deputy governor, the Reverend Increase Mather, a major who had resigned as a judge during the witch trials, and several other justices from various towns) signed a letter declaring their objections to the witch trials. The letter was written by Thomas Brattle, the same man who wrote earlier that the accusers had purposely injured themselves in court with pins and thorns hidden in their clothing. Brattle said that the group was "very much dissatisfyed with the proceedings; also several of the present Justices; and in particular, some of the Boston Justices were resolved to throw up their commissions rather than be active in disturbing the liberty of their Majesties' subjects, merely on the accusations of these afflicted, possessed children."

On October 19, a group of sobbing women reversed their previous confessions and revealed that not a single person they had accused of witchcraft had done them a bit of harm. They said their examiners had harassed them over and over to make them confess, and their families begged them to confess, too, so that they wouldn't hang. Finally they'd had no other choice than to wrong themselves and lie about their friends.

On Saturday, October 29, Massachusetts's Royal Governor William Phips put a halt to all further arrests and disbanded the notorious Court of Oyer and Terminer. He also released a lot of the people who were still in jail. On December 14, a brand new Superior Court of Judicature was established, though Chief Justice Stoughton and friends were still included. Their new job was to figure out what to do with accused witches who hadn't yet been tried. And this had to be done without basing any cases on spectral evidence; all those stories from the Invisible World had been banned at last.

The upshot was that out of 52 people tried before the new court in January and February 1693, only three were convicted, and each of them had already confessed. (This rule had changed, too. If you confessed, you no longer got off scot-free or received special privileges.) The governor later released all three anyway, and nine suspects who had been sent to jail earlier weren't even called into court. The Salem witch trials had ended.

We may never know exactly what caused the tragedy in Salem. The root of all this horror and pandemonium lies buried in a dark and misty past. Oh yes, every single sentence in surviving trial transcripts, every surviving letter written by eyewitnesses, each legal document, and all of the books written during the period have been scrutinized by scholars for well over 300 years. And yes, every new explanation about the cause of the dread disease or the motives of the accusers has been debated over and over again by professional historians. Some of the most well-known ideas have been ruled out, but even so, plenty of questions and theories still remain.

WHAT CAUSED THE FITS
AND THE HYSTERIA OVER WTICHES?

Was there really a dread disease running rampant in New England? If so, could it have been encephalitis or Lyme disease, both of which exhibit many of the symptoms described by the victims? Were any sick people and animals poisoned by hallucinogenic jimson weed or a fungus in rye called ergot?

Did people who had originally lived on the frontier during the Indian wars suffer from fits and see visions of

specters because they had post-traumatic stress disorder? After all, many members of their own families had been massacred right before their eyes. And did the Puritans' belief that Indians were devils and witches worsen their fear of attacks by unknown forces as well?

∽ WERE THE ACCUSERS CROOKED OR HONEST? ∽

Were the families of at least some of the afflicted simply trying to protect their loved ones from the Devil and his witches? That might make perfect sense because most everyone believed in witches and the Devil back in those days. And it does seem that some people and animals were really sick.

Was there an evil plot by Reverend Parris, Thomas Putnam, and their supporters to take advantage of hysteria over the dread disease by doing away with their personal enemies? Did the Putnams' jealousy and anger over the perceived loss of their property spur a desire to destroy the Porters' supporters by making them look like witches?

Rebecca Nurse's son and son-in-law and Sarah Cloyse's husband thought so, and they later helped force Parris to leave the community. And a series of letters and documents Putnam wrote or co-wrote in 1691 and 1692 indicate that he may have set up the accusations against Reverend George Burroughs, Burroughs's arrest, and his daughter Ann's testimony against the minister. He may even have worked with the judges to see that Burroughs was found guilty and hanged.

Was some of the witch hunting the result of that big fight between Reverend Parris and the members of his congregation who refused to pay his salary? These members had also been incensed over a 1689 contract with Parris that had given him the house he lived in. (Usually, the church would own the house, and the minister working there at the time would live in it.)

What about the testimony of the young girls? Had a group of them joined in a secret conspiracy to fake their fits and tortures? Did they purposely stick pins into their own skin during the trials or secretly bite themselves before accusing the witches of harming them? If so, why? Were some of them simply helping their parents by making their enemies look bad in court? Were they bored thrill seekers trying to get attention? Was it all a big game to pull the wool over the eyes of the adults? After all, John Proctor's servant Mary Warren, who had once accused the accusers of lying, reported that one girl said they went after the innocent suspects "for sport . . . we must have some sport."

WERE THE JUDGES CROOKED OR HONEST?

Were the judges, consciously or unconsciously, eager to put blame for their blunders during the Indian Wars at the feet of witches and devils to avoid responsibility themselves? Did they use the minister George Burroughs as their scapegoat because they disapproved of his unusual religious views? Or did the judges conspire to make off with a share of the arrested citizens' money and property. Three of the judges were related to George Corwin, the 25-year-old high sheriff of Essex County. They included the sheriff's uncles, Jonathan Corwin and Wait-Still Winthrop, and his father-in-law, Bartholomew Gedney. Sheriff Corwin was in charge of arrests and property seizures among other duties.

In those days, a witch's property was supposed to be turned over to the Massachusetts Bay Colony and the King of England after she or he was hanged. What's more, large fees could be collected from the accused witches and their families. But Sheriff Corwin ignored the King and the Colony and kept all that booty, even before anyone was hanged.

If certain judges connived with Corwin to convict wealthy people, maybe they got a cut of the action. Chief Justice Stoughton wrote out a warrant that allowed the estates and property of people who were executed to be seized and disposed of without ever telling Governor Phips or asking for his consent. This was illegal, too. And one time, when a Quaker woman asked why the court had seized her oxen, a judge replied, "Would you have us starve while we sit about your business?"

It seems likely that several of these theories are correct: Perhaps all of the disease, superstition, paranoia, hysteria, past resentments, cowardice, religious fervor, greed—and even boredom—boiled and bubbled together to foment a perfect storm in 1692 that finally exploded in the little town of Salem Village, to horrendous and tragic effect.

CHAPTER 10

WHAT HAPPENED NEXT

ven though the almanacs continued to predict rain and snow and phases of the moon, and even though Salem's town clerks still registered new births and collected taxes as usual, not all of the troubles came to an end once the witchcraft hysteria began to die down. Some people still thought the trials should continue. Others who had been afraid to speak up were mortified by the hangings. Newly freed "witches" and their families were embittered and impoverished. The church fell into disrepair due to lack of funds, and divisions among its members continued to fester. And despite Governor Phips's attempts to achieve a much wider peace with the French and Indians, the Second Indian War would grind on and on until 1699.

But when a 22-year-old Harvard graduate named Joseph Green was ordained as the minister of the Salem

Village Church in 1698, things began to look up. A natural negotiator, Green initiated a "Meeting of Peace" so that families who had left the church could reconcile with those who had stayed, and a sense of normality finally began to return.

Eighteen long years later, on October 17, 1711, the Province of the Massachusetts Bay signed a Reversal of Attainder, an act that declared a general amnesty and removed the witchcraft charges against George Burroughs and certain others. This was both good and bad. The good part was that it restored the rights and good names of some (but not all) of the living and dead "witches" and awarded some money to their heirs.

There were two bad parts. One was that the legislature only gave money to people who asked for it or whose names were included on a list that left lots of people out. The other bad part was that not one single person would ever be prosecuted for any of the crimes they had committed during the witch trials, whether they had falsely accused their neighbors of being witches, hanged the innocent, ruined their reputations, or stolen all of their property.

Meanwhile, here's what happened to a few of the people who were tangled up in witchcraft's wicked web.

✺ THE OFFICIALS ✺

Chief Justice William Stoughton

Stoughton believed he had done a great job of ridding the land of witches and was furious that Governor Phips had set them free. On January 3, 1693, he ordered the hanging of everyone who had been exempted because they were pregnant. But Governor Phips—whose wife was among those accused of witchcraft—blamed Stoughton for the entire tragedy and wouldn't allow him to hang the women. So Stoughton angrily quit his job as a judge.

Phips's slap in the face to the chief justice didn't hurt Stoughton's career one bit, though. When Phips was ordered to return to London later that year, Stoughton became the acting governor of Massachusetts, serving until his death in 1701 and even doing double duty as chief justice until 1699. He never once apologized for his role in the trials.

The Other Judges

On January 14, 1697, Judge Samuel Sewall took "the blame and shame" for his role in the witch trials and asked for the people's pardon. The same day, 12 other jurors signed a document apologizing for unwittingly shedding innocent blood, and the Massachusetts legislature declared the first annual Fast Day as everyone's penance for all the sins committed during the trials. Each year after that, Sewell made sure to observe a fast and to pray for forgiveness.

High Sheriff George Corwin

On May 15, 1694, Justice Stoughton's court helped out Sheriff Corwin once again by exempting him and his heirs from any liability for his failure to return all the goods he had stolen. Sheriff Corwin died at home of a heart attack in 1696. He was only 31 years old. Not one cent he extorted or stole from his innocent victims was ever turned over to the Crown, or the Colony, or the victims themselves during his lifetime.

❧ THE ACCUSERS ❧

Reverend Samuel Parris

Parris was the only person who offered any restitution to the accused witches and their families. In an attempt to keep his job by appeasing church members who had lost their loved ones because of the trials, he offered to subtract six pounds from his salary for 1692 and six pounds for 1693. The offer seems strange indeed: His total yearly salary was supposed to have been 66 pounds sterling (22 in money and the rest in provisions), but ever since 1691, the church committee had refused to pay him a cent.

In 1694, he apologized for his mistakes and tried to make peace with the congregation. Placing the blame on his servants and "Satan the devil, the roaring lion, the old dragon, the enemy of all righteousness," he said, "I do humbly own this day before the Lord and his people that God has been righteously spitting in my face."

But in the end, neither Parris's offer of restitution nor his apologies comforted his opponents. In fact, after Rebecca Nurse's son and son-in-law and Sarah Cloyse's husband directly accused Parris of destroying the innocent people in their families, they withdrew from his church. On May 3, 1695, 16 young men, 52 householders, and 18 church members sent a petition to Reverend Increase Mather and eight other area ministers, requesting that they advise Parris to quit and find a job someplace else. Parris refused, even though the ministers offered him a good job elsewhere if he would leave gracefully.

On July 14, 1696, Parris's wife, Elizabeth, died, but by

then most of the townspeople had lost all sympathy for him. Forced out of his job in 1697, he finally left town, but his reputation preceded him. Though he remarried and had two more children, the only jobs he could find were in the impoverished little frontier towns of Stow, Concord, and Dunstable. He died in Sudbury in 1720.

Betty Parris

 During the trials, Mrs. Parris had been worried sick about her daughter Betty's fits and absolutely refused to keep using the child to find witches. Toward the end of March 1692, Reverend and Mrs. Parris sent Betty off to Salem Town to live with Stephen Sewall,* Parris's distant cousin. Most of Betty's symptoms stopped practically right away, but not all of them. One night, Betty told Mrs. Sewall that "the great Black Man came to her and told her if she would be ruled by him, she should have whatsoever she desired, and go to a Golden City." New England Puritans believed that the Devil was dark skinned like

---

*Not to be confused with his brother, Judge Samuel Sewell.

the Indians. So Mrs. Sewall warned Betty that she had just seen the Devil "and he was a Lyar from the Beginning, and bid her tell him so, if he came again: which she did." In 1710, Betty married Benjamin Baron of Sudbury. She was 27 years old. Baron was a yeoman farmer, a trader, and a shoemaker. The couple had four children, one boy and three girls. We still don't know whether Betty was really sick from the dread disease back in 1692, though she was one of the two people who were most likely to have truly been ill. Did she ever admit, even to herself, the damage she had done when she testified against her slave Tituba and against her neighbors? We will never know.

Abigail Williams

Parris's niece Abigail stopped giving testimony against the accused witches by June 1692, long before the trials ended. Nobody knows why she disappeared from the hearings, but Abigail is the other accuser who may actually have been sick. She never did fully recover from the fits she had suffered and was no older than 17 when she died.

Ann Putnam Jr.

 When Ann was 19 years old, her parents died within two weeks of each other, and she was left alone to raise her nine brothers and sisters. Putnam never got married, but in 1706 when she was 29 years old, she asked to join the Salem Village Church. Always the peacemaker, Reverend Joseph Green offered his help. He guided her efforts to write an apology for lying in court, and he read it aloud in front of his congregation on August 25. Here's a part of her confession:

> *I desire to be humbled before God for that sad*
> *providence that befell my father's family; that I*
> *then being in my childhood should be made an*
> *instrument for accusing severall persons of a*
> *grievous crime, whereby their lives were taken*
> *away. I now have good reason to believe they*
> *were innocent, and I justly fear I have been*
> *instrumental with others, though unwittingly,*
> *to bring upon myself the guilt of innocent blood; I*
> *can truly say before God, I did it not out of any*
> *anger or ill will; but was ignorantly deluded*
> *by Satan. And as I was a chief instrument of*

accusing of Goodwife Nurse and her two sisters,
I desire to lye in the dust and be humbled for it,
in that I was a cause, with others, of so sad a
calamity; for which I earnestly beg forgiveness of
God, and from all those unto whom I have given
just cause of sorrow and offence.

Putnam was only about 35 years old when she died.

Mercy Lewis

 Mercy Lewis was still accusing people of being witches as late as January 1693. As she told it, one dark night when the moon slid behind the clouds, the spirit of Mary English had approached her to say the courts were about to free all the witches, so Mercy might as well become a witch, too, by signing the Devil's book. That way, his witches would stop afflicting her with such terrible fits.

Because Lewis was an orphan, she didn't have a dowry to offer in marriage. She apparently did get married at about age 27 though, but not before she had an out-of-wedlock child in 1695.

✎ THE INNOCENT ✎

Most of the accused witches who were still alive lost everything they owned. They lost their health. They lost their property. They lost their good reputations. And they lived in poverty. Once everybody in jail was finally acquitted, nobody could go home until they paid for their food and lodging. Now, how were they supposed to pay these bills if their farms had lain fallow because nobody was working the land, or if they couldn't work for wages while they were in prison? Some people had no way to come up with the money, and one woman named Lydia Dustin died in prison as a result. Here is the fate of some of the rest.

Tituba

 The person who probably spent the longest time in jail was Reverend Parris's slave Tituba. Parris had reneged on his promise to pay for her release, and she was locked up for about 13 months until a new master bought her for 7 pounds sterling around May 1693. This was quite a bargain. The average price for a slave fresh off of a slave ship from Africa that year was 26.02 pounds sterling. Tituba's unknown owner might have bought her husband, John Indian, too. There are no records to tell us what happened to either one of them after that.

Dorcas Good

Little Dorcas, the four-year-old daughter of convicted witch Sarah Good, had always been a perfectly healthy, normal child. But after she was shackled in heavy irons in a stinking, dung-filled, lice-infested stone prison for eight long months, and after receiving barely enough to eat or drink, and after being terrified by jailers and so-called witches and a slew of other criminals, and after she was coerced into accusing her mother of witchcraft, and after crying her eyes out when her mother was carted off to be hanged, and by the time a Salem man finally paid her bond so that she could be released from jail, it was too late. She had gone insane.

Sarah Osborn

Jail fever ran rampant among the prisoners, and at least six adults and one suckling infant died in prison. The infant was Sarah Good's other child.

Sarah Osborn, the sick old woman who was among the first three people accused of being a witch, died of the fever in prison, too.

Mary Watkins

In July of 1693, a suicidal maidservant named Mary Watkins was freed pending the payment of her jail fees. Watkins had been accused as a witch after she had accused her mistress. By July she didn't have a penny to her name and couldn't pay her fees, so when August finally rolled around, she was more desperate than ever to be free. Maybe Tituba's way out would work. She could file a petition to be sold! According to Robert Calef's written account, "She was continued for some time in prison, and at length was sold to Virginia," where she became an indentured servant.

Philip and Mary English and their Heirs

In 1693, wealthy Anglican merchant Philip English and his pregnant wife, Mary, came home to Salem only to discover that High Sheriff George Corwin had run off with everything they owned. There were no sheep on their land, no ships in their harbor, no family portraits in their parlor, and no wine in their wine cellar either. English was able to go back to his shipping business anyway since he still had a few ships hidden away at sea. But soon after she gave birth to a son, Mary died.

English filed claim after claim to get his property back, but when Sheriff Corwin died, the executors of Corwin's will gave English only 60 pounds sterling for items he had listed as being worth over 4,000 pounds sterling. In today's money, 60 pounds would be worth about $3,000, and 4,000 pounds would be worth about $200,000. But English's property was really worth considerably more money than that. Besides other items, English had originally owned 21 ships, not counting the ones that were hidden at sea. His stolen ships alone must have been worth an enormous fortune. English's heirs eventually received 200 pounds sterling from the General Court as tiny restitution for everything he had lost.

Elizabeth Proctor

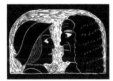

Sheriff Corwin's other victims received even less help than English. The prosperous Proctor family was completely ruined. After John was hanged, Elizabeth

Proctor was freed from jail with her newborn baby, but she never got one bit of their property back. A fake will disinherited her, and the court offered little help because she had been accused as a witch and was "dead in the law." It was not until December 1711 that the General Court granted Proctor's relatives 578 pounds and 12 shillings.

Mary DeRich

Rich people weren't the only ones who were robbed. Mary DeRich lost her bed and cooking pot—everything she owned—and she had no way to earn a living either.

The Family of George Burroughs

 When Burroughs was arrested for witch-craft in Maine, his third wife sold every single thing he owned, even the books in his library, and loaned out the money for interest. Then she fled with her own baby girl, leaving Burroughs's seven other children behind to fend for themselves without a cent. At the time, the oldest boy was only 16, wars were raging all around them, and the papers that proved they owned land in Falmouth had been burned along with the town. About 20 years after Burroughs was hanged,

130

the government awarded his children some money as compensation for his wrongful death.

Salem Village, Salem Town, and the Future

It would take another 300 years, but on May 9, 1992, the state of Massachusetts, the city of Salem, and the town of Danvers (originally known as Salem Village) finally dedicated a memorial in honor of the slain "witches." It is called the Salem Village Witchcraft Victims' Memorial of Danvers.

These days we can go to Salem for a Halloween extravaganza, a supernatural ghost tour, or a peek inside a witch's dungeon. We can visit accursed cemeteries and listen to scary tales (some true, some false) in a carnival setting where souvenir brooms and costumed witches abound. But never again will we allow witchcraft, the Devil, and the lure of superstition to rule the day in America.

OR WILL WE?

∽ NOTES ∽

Page 14 Devil, the leader of the Invisible World: Mather, *The Wonders of the Invisible World*, 95. According to Mather, the Devil was a black man who walked the streets with a chain lengthened by God so that he could move farther and farther to punish the wicked. His chain made a dreadful noise and brimstone made a "hellish and horrid stench in our Nostrils."

16 Disease in the New World: Perhaps 90 percent of the coastal Indians died from smallpox after settlers brought the disease to America on their ships. The Europeans thought the Indian deaths were God's will, since they meant that more land would be available for "civilized" European settlement.

17 "Here are but": Boyer and Nissenbaum, *Salem Possessed*, 175.

22 "under an Evil Hand": Norton, *In the Devil's Snare*, 19.

24 Witchcraft punishable by death: "Yf any man or woman be a witch (that is) hath or consulteth wth a familiar spirit, they shall be put to death." The Public Records of the Colony of Connecticut, "Capitall Lawes established by the Generall Court, the First of December, 1642," 77.

25 Tales in Mather's book: Linder, "Cotton Mather, *Memorable Providences*, Relating to Witchcrafts and Possessions (1689)." http://www.law.umkc.edu/faculty/projects/ftrials/salem/ASA_MATH.HTM

26 Cures with folk magic: In his 1651 book *The Art of Distillation*, John French tells how to distill snake and adder oil to cure deafness. His recipes for the cure of other ailments included the use of spirits from mummies or the brains of young men who had died violent deaths. And when people with rheumatism or other aches and pains added baked snails to a gallon of strong ale, they were cured—or so they thought.

27 "a-going to the Devil": *The New England Historical and Genealogical Register, April 1857, vol. XI*, 133

32 Examination of Sarah Good: Linder, "The Examination of Sarah Good, March 1, 1692." http://www.law.umkc.edu/faculty/projects/ftrials/salem/ASA_GOOX.HTM

41 Tipping point in witch hunt: "Once started, the alarm spread rapidly, and in a very short time a great number of people fell under suspicion, and many were thrown into prison on very frivolous grounds, supported, as such charges usually were, by very unworthy witnesses." Mather, *The Wonders of the Invisible World*.

42 "with all her naked": Roach, *The Salem Witch Trials*, 31-32.

43 Martha Cory's mistake: "By accusing her, the Putnams demonstrated that they would willingly attack anyone who openly questioned their motives and authority." Smith and Pollack, "Biography: Martha Cory."

43 "I know what": "Giles Cory and the Salem Witch Craft Trials," Cory Family Society. Last modified February 1, 2010. http://coryfamsoc.com/resources/articles/witch.htm

46 Ann testifies Cory prayed to Devil: Linder, "The Man of Iron: Giles Corey." http://www.law.umkc.edu/faculty/projects/ftrials/salem/gilescoreypage.HTM

51 "I can say before": Madden, "Examination of Rebecca Nurse of Salem Village."

51 "I cannot help": Ibid.

51 Church services: Former reverend of Salem Village Deodat Lawson would have said that the white angel was really the Devil: "Satan endeavours to Transforme himself to an Angel of Light, and to make his Kingdom and Administrations to resemble those of our Lord Jesus Christ." "A Brief and True Narrative by Deodat Lawson, 1692," in Burr, *Narratives of the Witchcraft Cases*, 1648-1706, 163.

52 "Oh! Her spirit..." Roach, *The Salem Witch Trials*, 71.

53 "a dead man": Boyer and Nissenbaum, "Letter from Thomas Putnam to Judge Samuel Sewall–Extract," *The Salem Witchcraft Papers*, 246.

55 Number of new accusations: "Before the end of April 15 new complaints were filed, doubling the number of accused witches in just 10 days. Between Monday May 2 and Monday June 6 another 39 people were charged." Norton, *In the Devil's Snare*, 122.

56 Witchcraft accusers and victim statistics: Roach, *The Salem Witch Trials*, Appendix B, 609-612.

56 Victims not officially listed: Norton, *In the Devil's Snare*, 321.

57 Dogs hanged: "Giles Cory and the Salem Witch Craft Trials," Cory Family Society. Last modified February 1, 2010. http://coryfamsoc.com/resources/articles/witch.htm

57 "scragged," "broken in her mind": Roach, *The Salem Witch Trials*, Appendix A.

60   "I am innocent": Ibid., 81-82.

60   "two men told": Linder, "The Examination of Bridget Bishop, April 19, 1692," http://www.law.umkc.edu/faculty/projects/ftrials/salem/ASA_BISX.HTM.

61   "He did torture": Boyer and Nissenbaum, "Deposition: Mercy Lewis vs. George Burroughs," in *The Salem Witchcraft Papers*, vol. I, 168.

61   "Because I am": Boyer and Nissenbaum, "Examination of George Jacobs, Sr. 10 May 1692," in *The Salem Witchcraft Papers*, vol. II, 474.

61   "bitch witch": Boyer and Nissenbaum, "Confession of Sarah Churchill," in *The Salem Witchcraft Papers*, vol. I, 211.

61 " You tax me": Boyer and Nissenbaum, "Examination of George Jacobs, Sr. 10 May 1692," in *The Salem Witchcraft Papers*, vol. II, 474.

63   "self-denying, generous": Linder, "George Burroughs." http://www.law.umkc.edu/faculty/projects/ftrials/salem/SAL_BBUR.HTM

64   "Oh dreadful! dreadful!": Woodward, *Records of Salem Witchcraft*, 109.

65   "Suspected to have": "Statement of Elisha Hutchinson" Essex Institute Fowler Papers Vol. 16, 11. Available online at http://salem.lib.virginia.edu/texts/tei/BoySal1R?div_id=BoySal1-n22.2&print=yes

65   "a Choice Child": Norton, *In the Devil's Snare*, 150.

65   "he was the Cheife": Boyer and Nissenbaum, "Elizar Keyser v. George Burroughs," in *The Salem Witchcraft Papers*, vol. I, 176-177.

66   "He told me": Woodward, *Records of Salem Witchcraft*, 114.

66   "immediately there appeared": Ibid., 109.

68   "could tell his thoughts": Ibid., 127.

70   "Mr. Burroughs carried": Ibid., 118.

77   "the awfull Frowne": Norton, *In the Devil's Snare*, 297.

78   "plumped or sunk": Nevins, *Witchcraft in Salem Village in 1692*, 151.

86   "When Witches were Tryed": Mather, *The Wonders of the Invisible World*, 215.

86   "At the time": Ibid., 215-216.

88   Nathaniel Saltonstall's resignation: "Giles Cory and the Salem Witch Craft Trials," Cory Family Society. Last modified February 1, 2010. http://coryfamsoc.com/resources/articles/witch.htm

90   "At the Trial of Sarah Good": Calef, *More Wonders of the Invisible World*, 357.

91   "No, I have none": Roach, *The Salem Witch Trials*, 107-108.

91   "If it was the last moment": Rosenthal, *Salem Story*, 101.

92   "I am no more": Linder, "Sarah Good," http://law2.umkc.edu/faculty/projects/ftrials/salem/SAL_Bgoo.HTM

92   Reverend Noyes's death: Scott, "Salem Witch Trials: The 20 Victims"

93   "If they were let alone": "Salem Witch Trials: The World Beyond the Hysteria," Discovery Education. http://school.discoveryeducation.com/schooladventures/salemwitchtrials/people/proctor.html.

93   John Proctor's petition: "SALEM-PRISION, July 23, 1692." (excerpt) "Reverend Gentlemen, our Accusers and our Judges, and Jury having Condemned us already before our Tryals, being so much incensed against us by the Devil, makes us bold to Beg and Implore your Favorable Assistance of this our Humble Petition, That if it be possible our Innocent Blood may be spared. We know in our own Consciences we are all Innocent Persons. Here are five Persons who have lately confessed themselves to be Witches, and do accuse some of us of being along with them at a Sacrament, which we know to be Lies. Two of the 5 are Young-men who would not confess any thing till they tyed them Neck and Heels till the Blood was ready to come out of their Noses. My son William Procter, when he was examined, because he would not confess that he was Guilty when he was Innocent, they tyed him Neck and Heels till the Blood gushed out at his Nose, and would have kept him so 24 hours, if one more Merciful than the rest, had not taken pity on him, and caused him to be unbound. They have already undone us in our Estates, and that will not serve their turns, without our Innocent Bloods. If it cannot be granted that we can have our Trials at Boston, we humbly beg that you would endeavor to have these Magistrates changed, and others in their rooms, hoping thereby

you may be the means of saving the shedding our Innocent Bloods. Desiring your Prayers to the Lord in our behalf, we rest your Poor Afflicted Servants. JOHN PROCTER, etc." Calef, *More Wonders of the Invisible World.* http://etext.virginia.edu/toc/modeng/public/Bur5Nar.html

93   "I fear not but": "Salem Village Witchcraft Victims' Memorial to Danvers," Salem Witch Trials. http://salem.lib.virginia.edu/Commemoration.html.

94   "It is a shameful thing": *Historical Collections of the Essex Institute*, Volume 3, 116.

94   Corwin stealing goods: Roach, *The Salem Witch Trials*, 237.

95   Noyes refuses to pray: Ibid., 242.

95   Petition for George Burroughs: Linder, "George Burroughs." http://www.law.umkc.edu/faculty/projects/ftrials/salem/SAL_BBUR.HTM.

96   "What I said": Hutchinson, *The History of Massachusetts Bay*, 493. Accessed via http://history.hanover.edu/courses/excerpts/244jacob.html.

96   Margaret Jacobs risks life: Compiled by T. B. Howell, Esq. *A Complete Collection of State Trials, Volume VI.* London: T.C. Howard, 1816, 665-666.

96   "with and for her": Norton, *In the Devil's Snare*, 256.

97   "The accusers said": Calef, *More Wonders of the Invisible World.* http://etext.virginia.edu/toc/modeng/public/Bur5Nar.html

99   "His tongue being forced": Ibid.

100   "the Devil hindered it": Rosenthal, *Salem Story*, 149.

100   "I Petition to": Boyer and Nissenbaum, "Mary Easty Petition," *The Salem Witchcraft Papers*, 304.

101   "Martha Cory, protesting": Calef, *More Wonders of the Invisible World*, 367.

101   Alice Parker: Scott, "Salem Witch Trials: The 20 Victims."

102   "the Devil hindered": Rosenthal, *Salem Story*, 158.

102   "What a sad thing": Hill, *A Delusion of Satan*, 188.

106 "It cannot be": Linder, "The Witchcraft Trials in Salem: A Commentary." http://www.law
.umkc.edu/faculty/projects/ftrials/salem/SAL_ACCT.htm

107 "better that ten": Mather, *Cases of Conscience Concerning Evil Spirits*, 66.

107 "very much dissatisfyed": Letter of Thomas Brattle, 77.

113 Theory of Putnam working with judges: Hill, *The Salem Witch Trials Reader*, 183.

113 "for sport": Hurd, *History of Essex County*, 1186.

115 "Would you have": Gildrie, *Salem, Massachusetts, 1626-1683*, 135.

118 Reversal of Attainder: Boyer and Nissenbaum, "Reversal of Attainder—October 17, 1711,"
Salem Witchcraft Papers, vol. III, 1017.

119 "the blame and shame": Roach, *The Salem Witch Trials*, 557.

121 "Satan the devil": Fowler, *An Account of the Life, Character, &c., of the Rev. Samuel Parris*, 15.

122 "the great Black Man": Lawson, *A Brief and True Narrative*, 160.

123 "and he was a Lyar": Ibid.

124 "I desire to": *The New England Historical and Genealogical Register, July 1858, vol. 12*, 246.

126 Average price of a slave: Derks and Smith, *The Value of a Dollar*, 28.

128 "She was continued": Calef, *More Wonders of the Invisible World*, 384.

129 English's property: English made an extensive list of hundreds of items stolen by Corwin
and then wrote: "The foregoing is a true Account of What I had Seized and Embezeld
whilst I was a prisoner in 1692 & whilst on my flight for my life besides a Considerable
quantity of household goods & other things for all which I Never Reseved any other
satisfacon for them Then Sixty Pounds 3s payd Me by the Administrators of George
Corwine Late Sherife desesd and the Estate was seisd & Tackin away Chiefly by the Sherife and his under offisers not withstanding I had given fore thousand pound Bond with
Surety att Boston." Boyer and Nissenbaum, *The Salem Witchcraft Papers*, vol. III, 991,
and Hill, *A Delusion of Satan*, 206.

✍ BIBLIOGRAPHY ✍

Boyer, Paul, and Stephen Nissenbaum. *Salem Possessed: The Social Origins of Witchcraft*. Cambridge, MA: Harvard University Press, 1974.

——. *The Salem Witchcraft Papers: Verbatim Transcripts of the Legal Documents of the Salem Witchcraft Outbreak of 1692*. 3 vols. Transcribed in 1938 by the Works Progress Administration under supervision of Archie N. Frost. New York: Da Capo Press, 1977. Available online at http://etext.virginia.edu/salem/witchcraft/texts/transcripts.html

Burr, George Lincoln, ed. *Narratives of the Witchcraft Cases*, 1648-1706. New York: C. Scribner's Sons, 1914. Available online at http://etext.lib.virginia.edu/toc/modeng/public/BurNarr.html

Calef, Robert. *More Wonders of the Invisible World*. In Burr, *Narratives of the Witchcraft Cases*, 1648-1706. Available online at http://etext.virginia.edu/toc/modeng/public/Bur5Nar.html

Demos, John Putnam. *Entertaining Satan: Witchcraft and the Culture of Early New England*. New York: Oxford University Press, 1983.

Derks, Scott, and Tony Smith. "Currency in Colonial America: Slave Trades 1600-1749." *The Value of a Dollar: Colonial Era to the Civil War, 1600-1865*. Amenia, NY: Grey House, 2005.

Discovery Education. "Salem Witch Trials: The World Beyond the Hysteria." http://school.discoveryeducation.com/schooladventures/salemwitchtrials/

Fowler, Samuel Page. *An Account of the Life, Character, &c., of the Rev. Samuel Parris, of Salem Village, and of His Connection with the Witchcraft Delusion of 1692: Read before the Essex Institute, Nov'r 14, 1856*. Salem, MA: William Ives and George W. Pease, 1857. Available online at http://books.google.com/books?id=bAIERsPLjmIC&source=gbs_navlinks_s

Gildrie, Richard P. *Salem, Massachusetts 1626-1683: A Covenant Community*. Charlottesville, VA: University of Virginia Press, 1975.

Hale, John. *Modest Inquiry into the Nature of Witchcraft.* Boston: B. Green and
 J. Allen, 1702. Available online at http://etext.virginia.edu/salem/witchcraft/ar-
 chives/ModestEnquiry

Hill, Frances. *A Delusion of Satan: The Full Story of the Salem Witch Trials.* New
 York: Doubleday, 1995.

——. *The Salem Witch Trials Reader.* Cambridge, MA: Da Capo Press, 2000.

Historical Collections of the Essex Institute. Vol. 3. Ed. John S. Pierson, A. M. Salem,
 MA: G. M. Whipple & A.A. Smith, 1861. Available online at http://www.archive
 .org/details/essexinstitutehi03esseuoft

Hurd, Duane Hamilton, ed. *History of Essex County Massachusetts. Vol. 2, pt. 1,*
 Philadelphia: J. W. Lewis and Company, 1888.

Hutchinson, Thomas, *The History of Massachusetts Bay.* 3 vols. "The Case of
 Margaret Jacobs." London: John Murray, 1828. Available online at http://history
 .hanover.edu/courses/excerpts/244jacob.html.

Karlsen, Carol F. *Devil in the Shape of a Woman: Witchcraft in Colonial New
 England.* New York: W. W. Norton & Co., 1998.

Lawson, Deodat. *A Brief and True Narrative by Deodat Lawson, 1692.* In Burr,
 Narratives of the Witchcraft Cases, 1648–1706. Available online at http://etext
 .virginia.edu/toc/modeng/public/Bur1Nar.html

Letter of Thomas Brattle, F.R.S., 1692. In Burr, *Narratives of the Witchcraft Cases,
 1648–1706.* Available online at http://etext.virginia.edu/toc/modeng/public/Bur1Nar.html

Linder, Douglas O. "Salem Witchcraft Trials, 1692." University of Missouri-Kansas
 City School of Law. Accessed 2009. http://www.law.umkc.edu/faculty/projects/
 ftrials/salem/salem.htm

Madden, Matt. "Examination of Rebecca Nurse of Salem Village." Undergraduate
 course paper, Salem Witch Trials Documentary Archive and Transcription Project,
 University of Virginia, 2001. http://www2.iath.virginia.edu/salem/people/
 nursecourt.html

Mather, Cotton. *The Wonders of the Invisible World: Being an Account of the
 Tryals of Several Witches.* London: J.R. Smith, 1862. Available online at
 http://www.archive.org/details/wondersofinvisib00mathuoft

Mather, Increase, *Cases of Conscience Concerning Evil Spirits Personating Men, Witchcrafts, Infallible Proofs of Guilt in Such as Are Accused with that Crime*. Boston: Benjamin Harris, 1693. Available online at http://etext.lib.virginia.edu/salem/witchcraft/speccol/mather/

Nevins, Winfield S. *Witchcraft in Salem Village in 1692: Together with a Review of the Opinions of Modern Writers and Psychologists in Regard to Outbreak of the Evil in America*. Salem, MA: Salem Press Co., 1916.

The New England Historical and Genealogical Register, April 1857, vol. XI. "Danvers Church Records." Ed. Samuel G. Drake. Andover, MA: Warren F. Draper, 1857. http://books.google.com/books?id=gWoFAAAAQAAJ&source=gbs_navlinks_s

The New England Historical and Genealogical Register, July 1858, vol. XII. "Danvers Church Records." Ed. Samuel G. Drake. Boston: H. W. Dutton & Son, 1858. Available online at http://books.google.com/books?id=q2oFAAAAQAAJ&source=gbs_navlinks_s

Norton, Mary Beth. *In the Devil's Snare: The Salem Witchcraft Crisis of 1692*. New York: Alfred A. Knopf, 2002.

The Public Records of the Colony of Connecticut. J. H. Trumbull and C. J. Hoadly, eds. Hartford, CT: Brown & Parsons, 1850. Available online at http://www.archive.org/details/publicrecordsofc001conn

Roach, Marilynne K. *In the Days of the Salem Witchcraft Trials*. Boston: Houghton Mifflin, 1996.

———. *The Salem Witch Trials: A Day-by-Day Chronicle of a Community Under Siege*. New York: Cooper Square Press, 2002.

Rosenthal, Bernard. *Salem Story: Reading the Witch Trials of 1692*. New York: Cambridge University Press, 1993.

Scott, Richard T., "Salem Witch Trials: The 20 Victims," Salem Focus. http://www.salemfocus.com/Victims.htm

Scottow, Joshua. *Narrative of the Planting of the Massachusetts Colony*. Boston: Benjamin Harris, 1694. Available online at http://digitalcommons.unl.edu/scottow/4/

Smith, Jillian, and Eliza Pollack. "Biography: Martha Cory." Undergraduate course paper, Salem Witch Trials Documentary Archive and Transcription Project, University of Virginia, 2002/2006. http://www2.iath.virginia.edu/saxon-salem/servlet/SaxonServlet?source=salem/texts/bios.xml&style=salem/xsl/dynaxml.xsl&chunk.id=b35&clear-stylesheet-cache=yes

Upham, Charles W. *Salem Witchcraft: With an Account of Salem Village and a History of Opinions on Witchcraft and Kindred Subjects.* 2 vols. Boston: Frederick Ungar, 1867. Available online at http://www.gutenberg.org/files/17845/17845-h/salemcontents.html

Warren, Charles. *History of the Harvard Law School and of Early Legal Conditions in America.* Vol. 3. New York: Lewis Publishing Co., 1908.

Woodward, William Elliot. *Records of Salem Witchcraft: Copied from the Original Documents.* 2 vols. Roxbury, MA: W. Elliot Woodward, 1865. Available online at http://history.hanover.edu/texts/salem/gburroughs.html

∽ INDEX ∽

As I sifted through volume after volume of research for this story, I was astonished by the vivid imagery that leapt from the pages of each and every trial transcript, letter, book, sermon, list of confiscated property, and other pieces of original source material related to the Salem Witch Trials. By sprinkling quotations from these writings throughout my book, I hope to transport readers back through time, to evoke the sense of horror and dread and wonder that made Puritan witch hunters and their victims pen their terrible words. But 400 years is a long time, and a living language like English has a way of shifting shape through the ages. So in order to clarify the quoted material for modern readers while still retaining its tone, I have abridged many long-winded passages, updated much of the spelling, and clarified a small number of the most archaic terms. To find the original texts, please refer to the notes.

Because this tale is so very dark in tone, and to echo 17th-century woodcuts, I decided to do the artwork in black and white with a few small red accents. I conjured up the pictures on Ampersand Scratchbord, a hard thin board covered with a layer of extremely white clay and then coated with black India ink. Making the artwork involves a labor-intensive process calling for a sharp pointed scratch knife that cuts away the black ink coating until a picture appears. The red accents are added by computer. To ensure the accuracy of my art, I referred to period works and photographs I took in and around Salem and Danvers, Massachusetts.

To see me working on the art for this book, scan this code or text Witches to 20583. To get a mobile scanner, text NatGeo to 20583. On your computer, go to YouTube.com and search for "Rosalyn Schanzer."